D0257523

CONTENTS

Start Here . . .

If this book has been bought for you in the hope of encouraging you towards the kitchen for reasons other than to retrieve a cool beer or ice for a gin and tonic, I trust that you will take the time to read it. You might be pleasantly surprised to discover a world beyond microwave meals and fish and chips. On the other hand, there is a chance that you have bought this book for yourself because you have a desire to learn how to cook. Or maybe you've got a hot date and all you can cook is fish fingers with chilli sauce. Perhaps your loved one has given you an ultimatum – either you start to help with the cooking or you do your own laundry. The book won't guarantee that you get your dream partner or manage to hold on to the one you've got, but it will teach you how to cook!

There are an awful lot of people out there who are struggling to get through the baked bean barrier. Fear not, help is at hand. Although this book will not turn you into the next 'super chef', it will teach you how to cook a variety of meals ranging from simple dishes, such as scrambled eggs, to others that are more elaborate.

Cooking is regarded by many as a chore, its purpose being purely to sustain life with as little effort as possible. Perhaps you rarely cook for yourself, preferring to rely on others or on takeaways or ready-to-cook meals. If you are one such person then it's time to change. Being able to cook is not solely a useful social skill. It should provide enjoyment and entertainment. Not only is it nice to cook *for* a partner but cooking together can be fun too. Another benefit from being able to cook is that, more often than not, it gets you out of doing the washing-up.

As you learn more about cooking you will begin to learn more about food. Most chefs are as passionate about the ingredients as they are about cooking them; inferior ingredients will normally result in an inferior meal. Cooking combines creativity, skill, timing and knowledge and the bonus is that you can eat the end result, which is one up on an oil painting! Alternatively you might not give a damn about how it looks provided it tastes good and there is plenty of it; each to their own. The intent of this book is simply to get you cooking, not to preach about etiquette and cuisine politics.

After a little use, you may notice the heavy influence of French Cuisine upon this book. There is a particular bias towards recipes from the Provençal region, where I have spent a great deal of time over the last 13 years. I have been fortunate enough to meet people who share my passion for food and who have taken the trouble to impart knowledge, enthusiasm and guidance on many of the famous dishes from the region. There is always something new to learn, and I continue my quest with an open mind and an open mouth prepared for my next culinary adventure.

The Rudiments

Being a good cook does not mean that you have to be able to create dazzling masterpieces every time you enter a kitchen. Learning how to cook is a gradual process that takes time and patience. Even the most experienced chefs have disasters. Remember that cooking is an art not a science. You will find that even when you follow a recipe word for word it does not always turn out the way it should. There are many factors that affect the final result and you have to be aware of this. If you repeat a recipe several times over it is unlikely that it will ever taste or look exactly the same. With experience you will learn how to adapt recipes to your own tastes and skills.

One of the best ways of improving your cooking is to watch other cooks. This is where you pick up the little tricks and secrets that will enable you to increase your knowledge and skill. Half the fun of cooking is in experimenting, using old skills and recipes and combining them with new ideas.

Kitchen Equipment

Any craftsman will have a set of tools that is essential to his trade. The same principle applies to the chef. There is a plethora of gadgets and gizmos on the market and it is very easy to believe that they are all essential. Only when you see your cupboards bursting with juicers, sandwich makers, blenders, steamers, yoghurt-makers etc that you realise you have little room left for the food. Although some gadgets can aid the chef – speeding up laborious tasks such as chopping vegetables – others are dispensable and will soon find their way to the back of the cupboard after the novelty has worn off. As a rule, it is far better to buy a few quality items than a number of inferior products. A frying pan that bends under the weight of a couple of sausages is going to be useless. Quality in cooking equipment often equates to weight, a pan should have a thick bottom and a sturdy handle. However this does not mean that a saucepan so heavy that you need to start body-building before you can pick it up, is necessarily going to be the best.

Kitchen Knives

Investing in a quality set of knives is essential. Very few people have adequate kitchen knives, often relying on blunt flimsy instruments that are potentially dangerous. When choosing knives bear in mind for which job they are intended. It is sensible to have a selection of different sizes; it is not easy using a 10-inch blade for peeling fruit. I generally use just two sizes, a small cook's knife with a 3-inch blade, and a large 7-inch knife. It is also useful to have a serrated knife for cutting fruit. If you have the choice between buying a cheap set of knives or a couple of high quality knives, go for the latter.

Freezer

If you are low on food or have an unexpected guest then don't panic; there should hopefully be something in the freezer that you can use. Or perhaps not. Do you actually know what is in your freezer and, perhaps more importantly, how long it has been there? It amazes me how many people's freezer contents lack any type of a labelling. It is often case of lucky dip and then trying to guess by touch what has been so carefully wrapped up, which is no easy task when the items are frozen. I have heard these mystery items referred to as UFO's (unidentified frozen objects).

So it is essential that your freezer is organised: this will save you time and money. Start by labelling and dating all the items in your freezer. It is also handy to keep a separate list on the outside of the freezer door which you can update every time you add or remove something. Bare in mind also that freezers run more efficiently when they are full, so try to keep your freezer well stocked even if it is half full of bread.

If you are going to make full use of your freezer then it is worth investing in a specific book that provides information on the different methods of preparing food for the freezer as well as telling you what can be frozen and for how long. Don't think that just because it is frozen you can retrieve a steak and kidney pie that your mother made for you in 1995.

Sensibility

The recipes in this book are created with simplicity in mind, both in terms of implements and cooking skills required. Cooking can be a very sensual experience with influences from both artistic and scientific domains. But don't forget that the element of common sense is the most important of all. I don't want to be held responsible for a person who ends up in the hospital burns department for having misunderstood the instruction 'stand in boiling water for 20 minutes'!

Another important point to remember is that all cooking times and temperatures are approximate. Not all ovens will take the same amount of time to cook a meal. If, for example, it is fan-assisted you will have to allow for the extra efficiency. Cooking is ultimately intuitive and no amount of instructions can replace this. Before you try any recipe read through it first to make sure you have all the ingredients and equipment as well as the time to prepare it.

The Kitchen

Just as a well-organised garage has a wide selection of high-quality tools and adequate working space, the same applies to the kitchen. The purpose of a kitchen is to prepare food, therefore the element of hygiene must not be ignored. If you are single then it is perfectly understandable to want to show your independence by being as messy as possible. However once you reach the stage of the overflowing bin surrounded by empty takeaway boxes you know it is time to consider clearing up.

The three main areas are organisation, safety, and hygiene.

Organisation and Safety:

• Keep heavy items in the lower cupboards.

• Never use a stool to stand on whilst trying to reach an object. Even a chair can be unstable. So ideally you should have a small kitchen step ladder.

• The kitchen should be well ventilated so that fumes and heat are removed quickly.

• There should be plenty of light, natural or artificial.

• A fire blanket and extinguisher should be kept handy.

• Keep cupboards tidy.

• Take care with the positioning of pans whilst cooking. Remember to keep the handles from protruding over the edge of the cooker.

• Make sure that handles on pots and pans are not loose.

• Keep an eye out for damaged flexes on electrical appliances such as toasters and kettles.

• Use caution when using electrical gadgets such as blenders and food processors.

• Keep matches and sharp knives out of the reach of children.

• Knives should be kept sharp, as a blunt knife can slip when cutting and cause an accident.

• Kitchen knives should be kept in a knife block. Keeping them in a drawer not only causes the knives to lose their sharpness, it also makes it easier to cut oneself.

• Never learn to juggle using kitchen knives. Old socks filled with rice make a safer alternative. Any type of rice will do, except egg-fried rice.

Fat Fires:

If you should experience a pan of fat igniting then remain calm and follow these rules.

• Never throw water on top of the oil – this will make it worse.

• Turn off the gas or electric hob if you can safely do so, otherwise wait until the fire has been extinguished.

• The most effective way to put out a fat fire is to get a dampened tea towel and place it over the top of the pan. Do not remove it for at least five minutes after the flames have subsided.

• If the fire is out of control, call the fire brigade and leave the house.

If you have children make sure they understand the kitchen is not an extension of the playground.

Hygiene:

Not wishing to get into the gory details, being violently sick is usually a consequence of bad hygiene. Harmful bacteria can spread quickly in the right conditions, so here are a few guidelines.

• All surfaces such as worktops, floors and cookers should be cleaned regularly, preferably every day.

• Never let your kitchen surfaces get cluttered. Clean up as you go along. This makes food preparation easier as well as reducing the burden of washing-up at the end of the process.

• Clean the door seals on fridges and freezers on a regular basis.

• Keep cooking utensils clean.

• Don't leave meat or fish out of the fridge for any lengthy period, especially if it has been cooked.

• Throw away food that is past its 'use by' date.

• Wash all fruit and vegetables.

• Make sure meat is sufficiently cooked. If you are having your meat rare, it must be as fresh as possible.

• Allow large pieces of frozen meat to defrost completely before cooking.

Weights and Measures

There are certain things that indicate our age. Comments such as 'during the war' and 'I remember when you could get a couple of lamb chops for a shilling', are a real giveaway. You might be asking what a couple of lamb chops and 'The War' have to do with food? Well not a lot, but somewhere in the mists of time the country went metric. Those imperial days are now long gone, but many people still prefer to think in imperial weights and measures, as I do myself. Hence the need to be able to convert metric to imperial and vice versa. Other amounts are referred to in spoons or cups which are self-explanatory.

The following abbreviations are used:

tbs = Tablespoon
tsp = Teaspoon

If you don't possess a set of kitchen weighing scales then it is possible to convert certain ingredients into spoon measures. Obviously the weights of all ingredients will vary, but here are some rough ideas . . .

1 tbs = 1 oz (25g) of . . . syrup, jam, honey
2 tbs = 1 oz (25g) of . . . butter, margarine, sugar
3 tbs = 1 oz (25g) of . . . cornflour, cocoa, flour
4 tbs = 1 oz (25g) of . . . grated cheese, porridge oats
All spoon measures refer to level spoons, not heaped.

1 tsp = 5ml
1 tbs = 15 ml
1 mug of rice weighs roughly 8 oz (225g)

The approximations used for conversion between metric and imperial in this book are as follows . . .

1 oz = 25g	2 oz = 50g
3 oz = 75g	4 oz = 100g
6 oz = 150g	8 oz = 225g
1 lb = 500g	
¼ pint = 150ml	½ pint = 300ml
1 pint = 600ml	2 pints = 1 litre

Gas Mark	°C	°F
1	140	275
2	150	300
3	170	325
4	180	350
5	200	400
6	225	425
7	230	450
8	240	475
9	250	500

Healthy Eating

Healthy eating is the bugbear of the late 20th and 21st century. Food gurus abound and every one of them has a different theory on what constitutes a 'healthy lifestyle': drink only water; eat only cabbage; low-cholesterol; hi-fibre.

However the simple key to achieving this state of heavenly dietry happiness is to adopt a *balanced* approach. Our bodies require certain elements (even fats) to remain in good working order.

Carbohydrates

These are the providers of energy. They also happen to be found in the cheapest types of food around such as bread, pasta, rice and potatoes. Although these foods are always available in ample supply, take care to limit your intake becasue an excess of carbohydrates can lead to obesity.

Fats

If you are confused by all the talk about different types of fats I will enlighten you. There are two basic types; saturated and unsaturated. The saturated fats are divided into polyunsaturated and monounsaturated. It is these saturated fats that are detrimental to our health. Too much saturated fat can increase the likelihood of heart disease as the arteries become clogged, thus impeding the blood supply.

Although we should not overdo fat intake we cannot do without it. Fat is an important source of energy for the body, but fats take longer to digest than carbohydrates. This means fat is useful for storing energy. It is present in a variety of products such as butter, margarine, milk, cheese and of course, meat.

By looking at the fat content on packaging you can see how much you are consuming. Low fat versions of many products are now available, although there is a tendency to regard them as an inferior substitute to the 'real thing'. More often than not it is a psychological mechanism trying to tell us that they don't taste as good.

Proteins

These are referred to as the 'building blocks' of the body. Proteins are produced from a combination of amino acids and are found in fish, lean meat, milk, cheese and eggs. Proteins are used to regenerate vital hormones such as insulin, adrenalin and thyroxin. A shortage of proteins results in poor growth or poor development of body cells.

Vitamins

This is one area where many people fail to supply their bodies correctly. The following are the most essential vitamins and their sources along with some of the maladies that are incurred as a consequence of the vitamin's absence.

Vitamin A

Vitamin A is present in dairy products such as cheese, butter and milk as well as in green vegetables and liver. It is needed for growth, and resistance against disease.

Vitamin B

Vitamin B is not one vitamin but a complex consisting of more than 16 different vitamins. They are to be found in whole grain cereals, liver, yeast, and lean meat.

Vitamin C
The main source of the vitamin is citrus fruits (for example lemons, oranges, and blackcurrants) and fresh vegetables. Vitamin C is needed for efficient functioning of the brain and nervous system. It also increases our immune response to infectious diseases including the common cold.

Vitamin D
A deficiency in vitamin D can lead to weak and brittle bones, a condition known as rickets, which predominantly affects children. In adults it can result in bow-legs. Thankfully this is a rarity now in this country. Vitamin D is found in milk, butter, cheese, oily fish and liver.

Vitamin E
This is a vitamin that does not usually pose a deficiency problem in our society. It is found in milk, cheese, butter and meat. One of vitamin E's most important functions is that it helps to keep the blood from coagulating, thus preventing internal blood clots.

Vitamin K
This is found in green vegetables. It helps the blood clotting process, which is useful after a cut.

Roughage
This is vital if you want to keep all your passages open, or if you are having trouble making substantial deposits. High fibre cereals provide a good source of roughage.

Water

It may seem obvious that the body requires a substantial amount of water in order to function correctly, but take this as a friendly reminder.

Minerals

There are three main minerals whose continued supply can all too easily be jeopardised: iron, calcium and iodine. Other minerals such as the phosphates, potassium, magnesium and sodium are generally in good supply.

Iron

This is vital for the formation of the red blood cells. If a person has a deficiency of iron it can lead to anaemia. This is a shortage of red blood cells. Women find they are more prone to this than men. Ensuring a high iron intake is not as simple as eating a bag of nails, however. Far better to eat liver, which is slightly more palatable, and is an excellent source of iron, as are other meats.

Calcium

This mineral is important for strong bones and teeth. It is found in dairy products.

Iodine

Iodine, although important, is not needed in the same quantities as calcium or iron. Fish is a good source of iodine.

Minerals and vitamins are available in pills from health food shops and supermarkets. Some contain multi vitamins, while others are more specific. It is still important to follow the recommended dosage.

Vegetables

Nutritionists are right when they say that we should increase the proportion of vegetables in our diets – unless we're vegetarian. Many people seem to have an adversity to anything that is healthy or fresh. In the past, the supply of vegetables was usually determined by what was available locally and according to season. However, supermarkets are now vegetable havens all year round, with exotic vegetables from the Far East alongside local produce. Although many of these imports are not cheap they do add tremendous variety.

There is still a tendency for people to overcook vegetables, which for me always conjures up a picture of school meals that would rather be forgotten. If you are cooking vegetables remember to measure their cooking time, don't leave them indefinitely. Vegetables taste and look better when cooked correctly and they retain more of their nutritional value.

Below is a list of some of the common and not-so-common vegetables currently available, explaining how they should be prepared and various methods of cooking.

Asparagus

This is not your everyday vegetable, but it is well worth splashing out on once in a while. Try to use asparagus as you buy it, don't keep it for days. When buying asparagus choose bundles that contain heads of the same size.

Untie the bundles. Remove 1 to 2 inches of the stalk. Using a small knife scrape downwards to remove the outer layer. Wash and tie back into bundles. Place the asparagus in a deep pan of salted boiling water and simmer for about 10 minutes or until tender. Serve straight away with either butter, mayonnaise or hollandaise sauce.

Aubergine/Eggplant

There are a number of varieties, but the most common are purple in colour. When buying aubergines choose those with a firm skin. Cut the top and bottom off and then slice thinly. Before cooking it is normal to extract the bitter juice that is present. Sprinkle lightly with salt and leave for 20 minutes. Before cooking, rinse the slices in water, then pat dry with a paper towel. The usual method for cooking aubergines is to fry them either in oil or butter until they soften.

Baby Sweetcorn

This expensive import from the Orient is worth the price. The only preparation needed is washing (don't forget behind your ears), following which they can be gently boiled or fried. To benefit from their full flavour they need to retain their crispness, so don't overcook.

Beans (French)

Wash them and top and tail. Cut into 1-inch lengths, or leave whole. Place in boiling salted water and cook for 10 to 15 minutes. After cooking they can be tossed in butter.

Broccoli

Wash in cold water. Cut off the stalks then divide into florets (clumps). Place in boiling water for about 10 minutes. Don't overcook as it will cause the broccoli to become mushy, losing most of its flavour and colour.

Brussels Sprouts

Remove the outer leaves and cut off the stalk (it should not be removed entirely, otherwise all the leaves will fall off). Cut a cross in to the base and then wash in cold water. Boil in water with a pinch of salt for 10 minutes.

Cabbage

Remove the rough outer leaves and the centre stalk. You can either shred or quarter the leaves. To cook the shredded cabbage place in boiling water for about 5 minutes. If the leaves are bigger they will need about 10 minutes.

Carrots

Top and tail the carrots and then either using a scraper or a knife remove the outer surface. Before cooking they can be quartered or sliced. Baby carrots can be cooked whole. Boil in salted water for 15 to 20 minutes. Carrots can be eaten raw in salads etc. They can also be roasted in oil when cooking a roast dinner.

Cauliflower

Wash in cold water and then divide into florets. Boil in salted water until tender – this should take about 10 minutes depending on the size of the florets. Cauliflower can also be eaten raw and used as a crudité.

Courgettes

Having been force-fed these for years I have almost come to like them. First of all give them a wash, then top and tail them. Slice thinly and fry in butter or oil for about 10 minutes. Alternatively boil for approximately 5 minutes.

Leeks

Remove the dark green section of the stalk and wash. They can either be sliced into rings, quartered or even left whole. To cook either boil for 10 to 15 minutes or fry in oil or butter for about 10 minutes.

Mangetout

If you haven't seen these before, they look like pea pods that have been squashed by a lorry. But they taste delicious and are arguably worth the extortionate amount you will be charged for them.

To prepare your mangetout, wash then top and tail them. If boiling, they need only 3 or 4 minutes because they maintain their flavour better when still crisp. They can also be fried gently in butter for a few minutes until they soften slightly. They make a colourful addition to stir fries.

Mushrooms

The many types of mushroom available range from the standard button variety to the more exotic oyster or shittaki. Some mushrooms can be eaten raw but always clean them first by wiping them with a damp cloth. Either remove or trim the stalk and then slice or leave whole. The mushrooms can be fried or grilled. To fry, melt a little oil or butter in a frying pan and cook for about 3 to 4 minutes, depending on size. To grill, put under a hot grill with a light covering of butter. Mushrooms can be a great addition to many sauces.

Onions

The best way to stop your eyes watering when chopping onions is to get someone else to do it. Top and tail the onion first and peel off the outer layer. It can then be chopped vertically or sliced into rings. Onions are normally fried in oil for about 5 minutes. They can be boiled in salted water for about 10 minutes. When frying onions take care that you don't burn them as this can taint a whole meal even if only a few of the onions are burnt.

Parsnips

Top and tail, then peel and chop into largish pieces or thick slices. They can be boiled, fried or roasted.

Place in boiling water with a pinch of salt for about 20 minutes or until they are tender. If they are to be fried they need to be cut into thin slices or chips, otherwise they will not cook all the way through. Perhaps the nicest way of cooking parsnips is to bake them. Place the parsnips in an ovenproof dish with a couple of tablespoons of oil, and bake in a hot oven for about 40 minutes. They can be basted as if they were roast potatoes.

Peas

If you have fresh peas, i.e. still in the pod, shell them and wash in cold water. To cook the peas, place them in boiling water for about 10 minutes.

Peppers

Available in red, green, yellow and orange. They all have different flavours – the lighter in colour they are, the sweeter they are; so the yellow ones are the sweetest and the green ones the most bitter.

Top and tail, then remove all the core and seeds. Slice into rings then halve and fry in a little oil for 5 minutes or so.
They can also be eaten raw and are particularly tasty in salads. Try one of the stuffed pepper recipes that are in this book as a third alternative.

Potatoes

Just as the Italians have their pasta, we seem to be mad about potatoes. We serve them in various guises, be it chips, crisps, roasted, boiled or mashed.

There are two basic types of potato: 'new' and 'old'. Both are available all year round. Allow 1 or 2 potatoes per person, depending on your appetite and the size of the potato.

All potatoes need to be peeled or scrubbed before cooking, unless you are preparing jacket potatoes.

Boiled:

After peeling or scrubbing the potatoes, cut into halves or quarters, depending on their size, then place in salted boiling water for 15 to 20 minutes or until they are tender all the way through.

Mashed:

If you want mashed potato make sure they are well cooked: you should be able to pass a knife through them easily. If they are not well cooked you find that the mashed potatoes have lumps in, however hard you try to remove them. Drain the potatoes, add a nob of butter and a drop of milk, then using a potato masher squash until they are nice and creamy, adding more milk and black pepper if required.

Roast Potatoes:

There are a number of ways to produce roast potatoes. Obviously having a potato and an oven is a good starting point. Peel the potatoes, then halve or quarter them depending on their size. Parboil for 5 minutes in salted boiling water, then drain. Drain the potatoes in a colander and shake so that the surface of the potatoes are slightly flaky (this produces crisp edges). Place the semi-cooked potatoes in a baking tray with some oil and place in the oven on Gas Mark 6 (425 °F, 220 °C) near the top of the oven if possible. Baste the potatoes with the oil a couple times while they are cooking. Roast the potatoes until they are golden and verging on crispiness, this should take between 60 and 90 minutes.

Chips:
These are a British institution, and they should of course be served with fish and wrapped in an old newspaper with lashings of vinegar and salt. If that description hasn't sent you running to the local chippy then here's how to make your own.

Peel some old potatoes and cut into chip shapes. If you are feeling sophisticated slice them thinner into French fries. The next stage is potentially dangerous so take care. The chips need to be covered (at least partially) in oil to cook, so a large amount of oil is needed.

Heat the oil in a large frying pan. To test if the oil is hot enough drop one chip in – if the oil bubbles loudly all around the chip it is up to temperature. Carefully add the chips, taking care not to throw them in the pan, otherwise hot oil will be splashed. Fry the chips until they are crisp, making sure that the oil does not get too hot. Remember to turn the heat off as soon as you have finished frying.

Pumpkin
If you have a whole pumpkin, cut it into 4 pieces then remove all the seeds and pulp from the inside. Remove the skin and cut into chunks. To boil, place in salted boiling water for about 30 minutes. After the pumpkin has been boiled it can be fried in butter for 5 minutes.

Spinach

When buying spinach, buy more than you think you need as spinach shrinks considerably during cooking. Discard any yellowed leaves, then place in a small amount of boiling water for about 10 minutes. Grated nutmeg and spinach taste good together.

Swede

Peel and chop into chunks, then wash in cold water. Cook in salted boiling water for 20 to 25 minutes or until tender. Can be mashed with a nob of butter and black pepper.

Sweetcorn

Remove the husks and the ends, then place in boiling water for 10 minutes. Drain, then serve with butter and fresh black pepper.

Tomato

Fresh tomatoes can be fried in butter, grilled or baked. To remove the skin of a tomato, which should be done when making sauces, place in boiling water for about a minute. Remove from the hot water and cool them in cold water. The skins should now come away with ease.

Turnip

Peel and cut into chunks, then place in boiling water for 20 to 25 minutes or until tender.

Stocks

Although it is easy to be tempted into using a stock cube, you'd be surprised how much tastier a recipe that uses fresh stock is in comparison, especially in soups and casseroles. Fresh stocks should only be kept in the fridge for a maximum of three days, but they are ideal for freezing.

Beef Stock

Ingredients

2 lb (1 kg) beef bones
1 tbs of oil
Water
2 carrots, peeled and chopped
1 onion, peeled and quartered
6 black peppercorns
1 bouquet garni
Salt

Heat the oil in a large pan, add the onions and carrots and fry for 5 minutes. After frying the vegetables, add the bones, peppercorns, bouquet garni and cover with cold water. Bring the pan to the boil slowly, removing any scum that will inevitably rise to the surface. A slotted spoon is useful for removing the scum.

After the stock has been brought to the boil it must be simmered for at least three hours, the longer it is simmered the more intense the flavour of the stock. Whilst the stock is simmering some fat will rise to the surface. This should be removed with a fat skimmer or kitchen towel. If the water level gets low add a little more.

Remove the pan from the cooker and strain. When strained, leave to cool and then remove any remaining fat from the surface

Court Bouillon

Court bouillon is traditionally used for poaching fish, giving a subtlety that is well worth the effort.

Ingredients

2 pints (1 litre) water
1 carrot peeled and chopped
1 stick celery, chopped
1 onion, peeled and sliced
8 peppercorns
1 bay leaf
¼ pint (150ml) vinegar
Salt

Place all the ingredients in a large saucepan, bring to the boil then simmer for about 20 minutes. Leave to cool before using.

Chicken Stock

Ingredients

1 whole chicken carcass
1 tbs of oil
1 onion, peeled and quartered
2 carrots, peeled and chopped
3 peppercorns
1 bouquet garni
Salt

Prepare the chicken stock using the same method as for the beef stock.

Savoury Sauces

There is the potential for an almost unlimited number of sauces, and they can be used to brighten up a plain-tasting dish or act as a harmonious accompaniment. Most sauces are based on a small number of elementary ingredients and once the fundamentals are mastered the possibilities are infinite.

White Sauce

This is one of the most used sauces to which other ingredients can be added.

Ingredients

¾ oz (20g) flour
½ pint (300ml) milk
I oz (25g) butter
Salt
Pepper

Melt the butter in a small saucepan, but don't let it brown. Then stir in the flour and cook gently for a couple of minutes. The combination of butter and flour is called a 'roux', and it is also the name of the method of preparation.

    Remove the roux from the heat and add a little of the milk. It has to be added gradually otherwise it will end up being lumpy. Stir the milk in until a smooth consistency is achieved, then progressively add the rest of the milk. When all the milk has been added return the pan to the heat and bring to the boil. Simmer for 3 to 5 minutes or until the sauce has thickened, stirring the sauce as it cooks. Season as required.

Cheese Sauce

This sauce is used in many of the recipes in this book, such as lasagne or cauliflower cheese.

Ingredients

½ pint (300ml) of milk
2 oz (50g) of grated cheese
¾ oz (20g) of butter
¾ oz (20g) of plain flour
Salt
Pepper

Repeat the method as for the white sauce, except after the sauce has been brought to the boil add the cheese. Stir in the cheese, then simmer until it has completely melted.

Parsley Sauce

Ingredients

½ pint (300ml) milk
¾ oz (20g) of plain flour
¾ oz (20g) of butter
4 tbs of chopped fresh parsley
Salt
Pepper

As White Sauce. The parsley is added just before serving.

Mayonnaise

Once you have made your own mayonnaise you will be loathe to return to the prefabricated variety: there is no comparison. There is even better news to come – once you have mastered making mayonnaise you can go on to make aïoli. This Provençal speciality is totally moreish, the only dilemma is that its main flavouring is garlic!

Ingredients

2 egg yolks
2 tsp of white wine vinegar
½ pint (300ml) of olive oil
Squirt of lemon juice
I tsp of smooth French mustard
Salt
Pepper

Put the egg yolks into a mixing bowl with the mustard and mix together. Then slowly begin to add the olive oil. The main problem with making mayonnaise is that it can curdle if the oil is added too quickly. Mayonnaise is time consuming to make and it is essential to take care. A fine drizzle of oil is needed and has to be controlled with total precision; hold the bottle of oil at the bottom in the palm of your hand, this gives more control. Using a balloon whisk, beat the yolks and the oil together, you will notice that the colour is quite yellow in comparison to the bought variety, but this is the way it should be. Keep whisking the mayonnaise until all the oil is added, then add the vinegar, lemon juice, salt, pepper and mix. Taste and adjust the flavourings to suit.

There is an alternative method. Mayonnaise can be produced in a food processor, but again fine control is required and the result is not as good. Put all the ingredients, bar the oil, in the processor and switch on, then add the oil slowly.

Aïoli

This is one Provençal recipe that lacks the characteristic vibrant colours normally associated with its cuisine. What it might lack in colour it makes up for in flavour – this recipe is a knockout. Aïoli should ideally be served with freshly-cooked vegetables such as courgettes or French beans and also tastes great with hard-boiled eggs and raw tomatoes. Serve on a large platter dish.

Ingredients

6 cloves of garlic
2 egg yolks
Juice of 1 lemon
½ pint (300ml) of olive oil
Salt
Pepper

Using a pestle and mortar crush the garlic with pinch of salt into a fine paste. If you don't have a pestle and mortar improvise using a small bowl and the back of a spoon. Transfer the garlic into a mixing bowl then add the egg yolks. The next stage is the same as when making mayonnaise; the oil must be added very slowly and be stirred constantly. When all the oil is added, season and add the lemon juice.

Tapenade

If you spend any time in Provence you are bound to come across certain dishes for which the region is celebrated and Tapenade is one of them. It is a paste that is named after the word Tapeno, which is French for capers. Should you ever be on holiday in the South of France and you wish to escape from the 'high life', take a trip down the coast to Cassis, which is close to Marseilles. Cassis is a small fishing port that remains unspoilt and oozes with charm. At the harbourside there is a terrace of restaurants that serve wonderful fresh fish. Alternatively sit in one of the cafes, sip a glass of Pastis or Bandol Rosé, nibble on a few olives and try some tapenade spread on toasted bread.

Serves 4

Ingredients

12 black olives, stoned
6 anchovy fillets
2 oz (50g) tinned tuna
3 tbs capers
1 clove garlic, peeled and crushed
3 tbs olive oil
1 tbs cognac

Put the olives, anchovies, capers, garlic and tuna in a food processor and blend to a paste. Then add the olive oil and cognac and mix well. The amount of olive oil used is only a guide-line, it depends on the required consistency as to how much is used.

Pesto

This recipe uses insane quantities of fresh basil, but the aroma is intoxicating. Pesto is traditionally served with pasta, but it can be spread on toast. It can be made in larger quantities and kept in a screw top jar in the fridge.

Serves 4

Ingredients

2 cloves of garlic, peeled and crushed
2 oz (50g) of pine nuts
2 cups of fresh basil leaves
3 tbs of finely grated fresh parmesan
¼ pint (150ml) olive oil
Salt

Put the basil leaves, pine nuts and the garlic in a blender and grind for a few seconds. Then add the cheese, oil and salt and mix well. If you are a stickler for authenticity, then you should prepare the pesto in a mortar, but a blender is far quicker.

Cranberry Sauce

Christmas. Humbug! I must confess to not being the biggest fan of Christmas. Too many relatives, silly paper hats, noise and commotion. Then there's the shopping. There are, I suppose, a few minor compensations; the inevitable repeats of Star Wars and Chitty Chitty Bang Bang to keep us amused, and an excuse to eat copious amounts of food, accompanied by attempts to drink the country dry. At the end of the festivities you are normally left fat, broke and with a hangover that will probably stay until the Christmas carols start playing in the shops reminding us that there are only 200 shopping days until next Yuletide.

Ingredients

8 oz (225g) fresh cranberries
½ pint (300ml) water
4 oz (100g) sugar

Boil the water in a large saucepan then add the cranberries. Cook for about 15 minutes or until they are tender. Stir in the sugar and heat through until the sugar has dissolved. If a thinner sauce is required add a little more water.

Barbecue Sauce

I tend to make barbecue sauces out of whatever is to hand. A little of this and that can provide some interesting results. Just remember to taste the sauce before you cover your meat or vegetables in it, as you could have concocted something awful.

Ingredients

4 tbs olive oil
1 tbs honey
2 tbs tomato purée
1 garlic clove, peeled and crushed
1 tsp tabasco
1 tsp Worcester sauce
2 tbs wine vinegar
2 tsp corn flour

Heat the oil in a small saucepan, then add the other ingredients stirring constantly. Make sure that all the ingredients are thoroughly mixed. Remove from the heat and cool. If you want to be a little more adventurous try adding other ingredients such as chutney, mustard, herbs or soy sauce.

Bread Sauce

No self-respecting turkey would be seen dead without the traditional accompaniments of bacon rolls, fresh cranberry sauce and of course bread sauce.

Ingredients

4 oz (100g) fresh white breadcrumbs
1 oz (25g) butter
¾ pint (400ml) milk
1 onion, peeled
4 cloves
4 peppercorns
Pinch of nutmeg
1 bay leaf
Salt
Pepper

Cut the onion in two and press the cloves into it. Place the onion in a saucepan with the milk, bay leaf, nutmeg and peppercorns. Bring to the boil then remove from the heat and leave to infuse for 15 minutes. Strain into a bowl then pour over the breadcrumbs. Mix in the butter then return to the pan and heat until the sauce thickens.

Mint Sauce

Ingredient

Cup of fresh mint
2 tbs vinegar
2 tbs castor sugar
2 tbs hot water

Wash the mint then remove the leaves. Finely chop the leaves and place in a bowl with the sugar. Pour on the hot water and stir. Leave for 5 minutes or until the sugar has dissolved. Add the vinegar and leave to infuse for at least 2 hours.

Apple Sauce

The perfect accompaniment to roast pork.

Ingredients

I lb (500g) cooking apples, peeled, cored, sliced
3 tbs of water
Juice of half a lemon
½ oz (15g) butter
2 tsp of sugar

Put the apples in a saucepan with the lemon juice, water, sugar and butter and simmer gently until the apples are soft. Take care not to burn the apples. If you want a smooth sauce put the mixture in a blender for a minute. If the sauce is too bitter add a little more sugar. To make the sauce a little special add a tablespoon of calvados.

Dressings

The use of dressings can add life to even the most miserable salad. By making your own dressings you can fine-tune them according to your own personal tastes. It should be remembered that a dressing should not swamp a salad. The salad should be coated not bathed. It is possible to buy ready prepared dressings but they rarely match those that are homemade.

French Dressing

Most people are familiar with French dressing, also commonly referred to by the French name vinaigrette.

There are many variations of French dressing, and most people have there own favourite combinations. Oil and vinegar are the primary ingredients to which herbs or flavourings can be added. Olive oil is a must for an authentic-tasting dressing – vegetable oil, although much cheaper, will not taste the same; and use a wine vinegar not malt. As with most recipes, even ones that only contain two ingredients, there are disagreements as to the correct proportions of oil and vinegar. This is yet another one of those daft arguments, the proportions should be based upon personal preference. In theory the average is 4 parts oil to 1 part vinegar. I'm not advocating this, you might prefer a less acidic flavour and use 6 parts oil, and so on.

Ingredients

4 tbs olive oil
I tbs white wine vinegar
Salt
Pepper

What could be easier? Put the oil, vinegar, salt and pepper in a small screw top jar and shake until the two liquids have combined. After a while the oil and vinegar will separate again.

If you want a dressing out of the ordinary try adding a little mustard or fresh herbs such as basil, mint, parsley or chives. An alternative to using vinegar is to use lemon juice.

Garlic Dressing

Make as above, but add half a finely crushed clove of garlic.

Yoghurt Dressing

Ingredients

¼ pint (150ml) of plain yoghurt
I tbs of lemon juice
Salt
Pepper

Mix the yoghurt and lemon juice together, season according to taste.

Dips and Savoury Butter

Humous

This is a dip of Middle Eastern origin and is easy to make. Although humous is available ready-made, it is cheaper to make your own. Having said that, I find it easier to use canned chick peas instead of soaking dried ones for hours. Serve with pitta bread.

Note that a blender is needed for this recipe.

Serves 4

Ingredients

1 can of chick peas
2 cloves of garlic, peeled and finely chopped
1 tbs of tahini
Juice of one lemon
2 tbs of olive oil
½ tsp of ground cumin
Paprika

Put all the ingredients in a blender and let them have it! Switch off when a smooth consistency has been achieved. Then put in a dish and chill for an hour or two. Before serving dust with paprika.

Serve with pitta or french bread.

Cucumber Raita

Serves 2 to 4

Ingredients

½ cucumber, peeled and chopped into pieces
A small pot of natural yoghurt
1 tbs of olive oil
1 tbs of freshly chopped mint
Pepper
Salt

Mix the cucumber, yoghurt and mint together in a bowl, pour the oil on top, and season.

Guacamole

Serves 3 to 4

Ingredients

2 ripe avocados
3 tbs lemon juice
1 tbs olive oil
1 clove of garlic, peeled and crushed
Pinch of chilli powder
Salt
Pepper

Peel the avocados and remove the stones. Mash the flesh with a fork and add the other ingredients. Season to taste and serve with tortilla chips, raw vegetables or on toast.

Starters

If you are going all out to impress then a pair of clean socks, an ironed shirt and a shave are a step in the right direction. Don't stop there, however. Should you want to create a special meal, make the effort to produce a starter.

Deep Fried Camembert

Serves 2

Ingredients

Vegetable oil
1 Camembert cheese
Dried white breadcrumbs
1 egg, beaten

Cut the Camembert into four then dip in the egg, followed by a roll in the breadcrumbs, making sure they are evenly coated. Put on a plate and place in the fridge for 30 minutes.

Heat the oil in deep fryer until it begins to smoke. Test the temperature by dropping a breadcrumb into the oil, it should sizzle as soon as it hits the surface. When the oil is at the correct temperature fry the Camembert until golden. Drain and then serve with redcurrant sauce.

Alternatively, if you are having a barbeque, why not wrap a whole Camembert in foil and place it in the embers of the fire?

Smoked Salmon Salad

Serves 4

Ingredients

Mixed salad
4 oz (100g) smoked salmon
Lemon
Salt
Pepper
Olive oil

Arrange the salad on four small plates, so that the plate is covered with salad. Cut the salmon into small pieces then place on the salad. Drizzle lightly with olive oil then season. Serve with lemon wedges.

Moules Marinières

Serves 4

Ingredients

4lb (2kg) mussels
2 cloves of garlic, peeled and finely chopped
4 shallots, peeled and finely chopped
2 tbs of chopped parsley
1 oz (25g) butter
1 pint (600ml) of white wine
1 bouquet garni
Salt
Pepper

Scrub the mussels and remove the beards that are usually attached to them. If there are any mussels that are already open or cracked discard them. Put the shallots, wine, garlic and parsley into a large saucepan and simmer for 5 minutes. Add the mussels and the bouquet garni, turn up the heat and cook for about 5 minutes. Then add the butter and cook for another 10 minutes. Whilst the mussels are cooking shake the pan a couple of times, this helps the mussels to open and ensures they are cooked evenly.

When cooked, remove the bouquet garni and any mussels that have not opened. Season and then serve with the juice. If a slightly stronger tasting sauce is required, reduce the sauce by boiling it rapidly for a few minutes. The mussels should be served immediately with a little chopped parsley on top.

Garlic Bread

Serves 4

Ingredients

French stick
4 oz (100g) of butter
2 cloves of garlic

Put the butter in a small mixing bowl. Finely chop the garlic and add to the butter, blending it in with a fork. Slice the French stick at 2-inch intervals, without actually severing it, and spread some of the butter on both sides of each slit. Then close up the gaps and wrap the loaf in foil. Place in the oven and cook for 15 to 20 minutes at Gas Mark 5 (400 °F, 200 °C).

Mini Sausages with Honey and Rosemary

Serves 4

Ingredients

Pack of mini sausages
Handful of fresh rosemary
3 tbs of runny honey

Arrange the sausages in a baking dish, prick with a fork, spoon
on the honey, then place the rosemary on top. I find that slightly
crushing the rosemary gives a stronger taste to the sausages.
Bake in the oven on Gas Mark 6 (425 °F, 220 °C) for about 40
minutes, turning occasionally so they brown evenly. If you are
in a hurry stick the sausages under the grill.

Mushrooms with Garlic Butter

Serves 4

Ingredients

4 oz (100g) of mushrooms
3 oz (100g) of butter
2 cloves of garlic, peeled and finely chopped

Remove the stalk of the mushrooms then wash. Mix the butter
and the garlic together with a fork and then spread on top of
the mushrooms. Bake in the oven for 15 minutes on Gas Mark
5 (400 °F, 200 °C).

Soups

The recipes for soup are legendary. There are thick, thin, clear, hot and cold ones. It is possible to produce soup from almost any natural ingredients. A blender is essential if you want a smooth soup. Soups are ideal for freezing so why not make double the quantity and freeze what you don't use?

Carrot And Ginger Soup

Sometimes known as 'Jasper and Rogers Soup', though not very often. This is my favourite of all soups, the ginger gives it a delicious flavour that never fails to impress. Use fresh ginger, but remember to take it out before serving.

Serves 4

Ingredients

1 lb (500g) carrots, peeled and chopped
1 potato, peeled
1 piece of fresh root ginger, peeled and chopped
2 pints (1 litre) water
4 tbs single cream (optional)
Salt
Pepper

Place the carrots, potato and ginger in a pan and cover with the water. Bring to the boil and then simmer for 20 minutes. Remove from the heat and take out the ginger. Transfer the ingredients into a blender and blend until a smooth consistency is achieved. Season according to taste and stir in the cream if desired.

Tomato Soup

Still one of the most popular soups. Why not try spicing it up by adding a few pinches of chilli powder?

Serves 4

Ingredients

1 lb (500g) of tomatoes
1 onion, peeled and finely chopped
1 clove of garlic, peeled and chopped
 1 bouquet garni
1 pint (600ml) of water
½ pint (300ml) of milk
1 tbs of oil
Salt
Pepper

Boil some water in a saucepan, then place the tomatoes in it. Remove the pan from the heat and leave for about 5 minutes. Take the tomatoes from the water and peel off the skins. Chop into small pieces.

Fry the tomatoes and garlic and onions gently in the oil for about 15 minutes until they go mushy. Add the water and bouquet garni, then simmer for 1 hour. If you don't want bits in your soup you can sieve it. Otherwise, just add the milk to the tomato mixture and stir. Season. Simmer for about 3 minutes, then serve.

French Onion Soup

The French are passionate about their soups and most regions have their own speciality which reflects the area, the climate and the produce. With this recipe there are no firm rules and numerous variations on the same theme occur. This is one soup that benefits from using homemade beefstock.

Serves 4

Ingredients

2 large onions, peeled and thinly sliced
2 pints (1 litre) of beef stock
2 tsp flour
1 tbs oil
4 slices French bread
2 oz (50g) Gruyère cheese, grated
Salt
Pepper

Heat the oil in a saucepan, then fry the onions slowly for 15 minutes, until they end up a golden colour. Stir in the flour and cook for about 5 minutes, stirring the onions constantly. Add the beef stock and bring to the boil. Season and simmer for 25 minutes. About 10 minutes before it is cooked, preheat the grill. Divide the cheese onto the slices of bread. When the soup is ready pour it into a serving dish, (to be authentic you should have an earthenware tureen). Place the slices of bread on top of the soup and place under the grill until the cheese melts.
    Serve immediately.

Vegetable Soup

At the end of the summer there is usually an abundance of fresh vegetables available from local nurseries. I buy vast quantities of tomatoes and make up batches of tomato sauce and soup that can be frozen and used when needed during the winter. There are no limits as to which vegetables you can use. This is just a guideline.

Serves 4

Ingredients

2 tbs of oil
1 onion, peeled and chopped
1 leek, thinly sliced
2 cabbage leaves, shredded or finely chopped
1 courgette, finely chopped
1 carrot, scraped and sliced
1 tsp mixed herbs
1 bay leaf
2 pints (1 litre) of vegetable stock
Salt
Pepper

Heat the oil in a large saucepan, then fry the onions for about 5 minutes or until they have softened. Add the other vegetables and fry for a further 10 minutes. Add the stock and herbs then season. Bring to the boil, then simmer for 30 minutes. Remove the bay leaf before serving. If you want a smoother textured soup then liquidise before serving.

Curried Parsnip and Apple Soup

A liquidiser is required for this recipe.

Serves 4

Ingredients

2 tbs of oil
I large onion, peeled and chopped
I ½ lb (750g) parsnips, peeled and chopped
I apple, peeled and cored
2 tsp medium curry powder
2 pints (I litre) of vegetable stock
Salt
Pepper

Heat the oil in a large saucepan, then fry the onions and curry powder for about 5 minutes until they have softened. Add the apple and the parsnips and fry gently for another 5 minutes. Stir in the stock and bring to the boil, then simmer for 30 minutes. Transfer the soup into a liquidiser and blend until smooth.

Serve with fresh crusty bread. If you don't like the flavour of curry then omit it.

Gazpacho

This is a thin chilled soup that is a very refreshing on a hot summer's evening. A blender is needed for this recipe. I often add a dash of tabasco sauce, but this is optional.

Serves 4

Ingredients

8 oz (225g) ripe tomatoes, skinned
½ green pepper, deseeded and chopped
½ red pepper, deseeded and chopped
½ cucumber
1 pint (600ml) of tomato juice
1 onion, peeled and chopped
1 clove of garlic, peeled and chopped
2 tbs of olive oil
1 tbs tarragon vinegar
1 tbs of fresh chives
1 tbs of fresh parsley
Salt
Pepper

Chop all the vegetables into chunks and put aside a little of each for the garnish. Place all the ingredients except for the oil into a blender for 2 minutes or so. Then add the oil and seasoning, place in the fridge for at least 3 hours. A few ice cubes can be added to speed up this process, but don't add too many as it will make the soup weak. Serve with the remaining vegetables on top.

Chilled Cucumber Soup

This is another soup that is ideal for serving during the summer months.

Serves 4

Ingredients

2 cucumbers, peeled and sliced
1 tbs of flour
1 pint of chicken stock
½ pint (300ml) of water
½ tsp of grated nutmeg
¼ pint (150ml) of single cream
1 bay leaf
1 tbs fresh mint, chopped
Salt
Pepper

Place the cucumber in a saucepan with the water and cook until tender. Remove from the heat, drain and then put in a blender for a minute or two until smooth. Return the cucumber to the saucepan and stir in the flour. Add the stock, seasoning and bayleaf and slowly bring to the boil. Simmer for 5 minutes then cool and strain. Once strained stir in the cream and chill in the fridge for a couple of hours. When you feel thoroughly chilled, get out of the fridge and serve the soup with a decoration of mint.

Pumpkin Soup

This recipe requires a liquidiser and a little enthusiasm for Hallowe'en. The soup tastes best through a witch's mask, but a goblin's will suffice.

Serves 4

Ingredients

1 ½ lb (750g) of pumpkin flesh, cut into cubes
½ pint (300ml) of milk
4 oz (100g) of butter
Salt
Pepper

Melt the butter in a saucepan, then fry the pumpkin until it is soft and mushy. Season, then add milk and put into a liquidiser for a minute. Put the liquid back into a saucepan and heat through, but do not boil.

Salads

Thankfully the days are long gone when a salad consisted only of a limp lettuce leaf, a tomato and a few crinkled slices of cucumber. There is an increasingly exotic selection of salad vegetables available: some supermarkets stock up to ten different varieties of lettuce alone. Salads are still more popular during the summer months when the produce is cheaper.

Alsace Salad

This is of my favourite salads. Appetites tend to be large in this region of France and being close to the border with Germany much of the cuisine is under the influence of both countries. This is not the region to visit if you are attempting to lose weight.

Serves 2

Ingredients

1 lettuce
4 rashers of bacon, cut into pieces
2 eggs
2 tomatoes, quartered
2 tbs of oil
Salt
Pepper

Heat the oil in a frying pan and fry the bacon. With this particular recipe the bacon pieces need to be verging on crispness, but don't let them burn. When they are cooked put them aside in a separate dish or bowl. Clear the pan of any debris then fry the eggs. Whilst the eggs are cooking arrange the lettuce in a serving dish with the tomatoes and the bacon. When the eggs are cooked let them cool for a minute and then place on top of the salad, then season.

Cucumber Salad

Serves 4

Ingredients

1 large cucumber
1 tbs white wine vinegar
1 tsp sugar
1 tbs olive oil
2 tbs chopped fresh chives
Salt
Pepper

Peel the cucumber and slice as thinly as possible.

Arrange the slices of cucumber on a flat plate and sprinkle generously with salt. Place another plate of a similar size on top and press down gently.

Leave in the fridge for 1 hour. Remove from the fridge and pour away the water that has been extracted. Mix the vinegar, oil and sugar together, then pour over the cucumber. Season, then sprinkle the chopped chives on top

Tomato and Onion Salad

A typical Provençal salad, so popular that anyone indigenous to the area would give their best goat for just a taste of it (the salad, not the goat). There is no need to carry any cash with you when you travel in Provence, just arm yourself with a few of these salads and you will soon find yourself with more goats than you know what to do with.

Serves 4

Ingredients

4 fresh tomatoes
1 onion
Fresh basil
Pepper
Salt
French dressing

Peel the onion and slice fairly thinly. Slice the tomatoes and arrange them on a large plate or dish. Place the onion pieces between the tomato slices. Decorate with the basil leaves, and season with plenty of freshly ground pepper. Pour the French dressing over the top.

Salad Niçoise

This salad is legendary in Provence, and is still popular in both restaurants and the home. As with many French recipes there are numerous variations on the same theme. So there is never a 'right' way!

Serves 4

Ingredients

1 lettuce
3 ripe tomatoes
10 French beans cooked and cooled
3 eggs
8 oz (225g) tin of tuna
Small tin of anchovies
10 olives
French dressing

Hard boil the eggs for 8 minutes, then place in a bowl of cold water. Wash the lettuce and arrange the leaves in a large serving bowl, then add the tuna (drain the oil first) and toss it all together.

Quarter the tomatoes and place them on top of the lettuce, with the beans. Shell the eggs, cut them into quarters, and arrange them neatly on top. Pour the dressing over the salad, and add the olives and anchovies, if required. Other ingredients that are sometimes used include radishes and peppers.

Italian Pepper Salad

There are many ways of serving peppers but this simple recipe is one of the best.

Serves 4

Ingredients

4 large peppers (mixture of colours)
4 tbs of olive oil
Salt
Pepper

Heat the oven to the highest setting possible and then place the peppers on a tray on the top shelf. They should stay in the oven for about 20-30 minutes after the oven is up to temperature. After about 15 minutes turn the peppers over so they are evenly cooked.

Remove from the oven and put the peppers in a clean polythene bag and tie the ends together. Leave the peppers in the bag for at least 15 minutes then remove and peel off the skins. Make sure all the skin is removed, as it is burnt, it has a very strong flavour and can taint the dish.

After removing the skin, the stems and the seeds, cut into strips. Place the peppers in a serving dish, drizzle with the oil and then season. There will normally be some residue from the peppers in the polythene bag that can be added to the dish for extra flavour.

Tomato and Feta Salad

Serves 4

Ingredients

6 ripe tomatoes
4 oz (100g) feta cheese
10 black olives
Olive oil
Salt
Pepper

Slice the tomatoes and arrange on flat plate or platter dish. Cut the cheese into cubes or crumble into small pieces and place on top of the tomatoes. Arrange the olives on top, season, then drizzle with oil.

Pasta Salad

Serves 3 to 4

Ingredients

4 oz (100g) of pasta quills or shells
½ red pepper, deseeded and chopped
½ green pepper, deseeded and chopped
8 oz (225g) tin of tuna
3 tomatoes, sliced
3 tbs double cream
Pepper

Boil some water in a saucepan and cook the pasta for about 15 minutes or until it is tender, then drain.

Drain the oil from the tuna then mix all the ingredients together in a serving bowl and season.

Tabbouleh

Bulghur wheat is made from wheat that has been boiled, dried, then ground. As an ingredient it is widely used in countries like Morocco and Tunisia.

Serves 4

Ingredients

6 oz (150g) of bulghur wheat
1/8 pint (60ml) of olive oil
½ cucumber, chopped
2 tomatoes, peeled and chopped
1 bunch of spring onions
1 bunch of parsley
8 mint leaves, chopped
Juice of one lemon
Salt
Pepper

Place the bulghur wheat in a saucepan of water. Bring to the boil, then simmer gently for 10 to 15 minutes until tender. Drain, then allow to cool.

Finely chop the parsley and the spring onions. Place the bulghur in a serving bowl, add the olive oil, parsley, mint, tomato, cucumber, spring onions, lemon juice, salt and pepper. Mix together thoroughly.

Goat's Cheese Salad

Even if you are into strong cheese, a ripe goat's cheese can bring tears to your eyes. There are many ways of serving goat's cheese, apart from the obvious bread accompaniment. It is sometimes served with fresh figs, or in a salad.

Serves 4

Ingredients

4 small goat's cheeses
Mixed salad
2 tbs of olive oil
Salt
Pepper

Arrange the salad on four small plates. Heat the oil in a small frying pan and then add the cheese. Lightly fry the cheese until it gets close to melting. Use a pan slice to remove it from the pan and then place on top of the salad. Any oil that remains in the pan can be poured over the salad. Finally season.

Choosing Meat

Although there are many tantalising and of course healthy vegetarian meals, the allure of meat is often too strong to ignore. A fillet steak cooked to perfection with a green salad and French fries is absolutely delicious.

Cooking Meat

There are a number of methods for cooking meat, including grilling, frying, stewing and roasting. The decision as to which method is chosen depends on the type of meat being used, the flavour required and also health considerations.

Grilling

As the grilling process does not tenderise meat it is important to remember that only tender meat should be grilled. When grilling chops or steak, preheat the grill for at least 10 minutes. Grilled meats should be browned on the surface but succulent in the middle. One of the advantages of grilling is that it requires little or no fat, making it one of the healthiest methods of cooking.

Frying

There are two basic methods of frying, determined by how much fat is used – shallow or deep-fat.

One of the advantages of frying is that the juices and the natural fats are kept in the pan and add to the flavour of whatever is being cooked, they can also be used as a basis for sauces. When grilling meat the juices are lost in the bottom of the grill pan.

Roasting

Still a popular method and quite rightly so. A variety of meats can be roasted and they are usually basted in their own juices and fat. Less tender cuts of meat should be roasted more slowly. Joints should be basted every 20 minutes.

Deep frying

Special deep fryers can be purchased. Failing that use a frying pan with deep sides. Deep frying is a very quick method of cooking meat, but this method of cooking is better suited to batters or fries.

Stewing

This method is ideally suited for meat that is not particularly tender. Stewing normally involves cooking slowly in a liquid. There are two types of stew, brown and white. A brown stew is where the meat is browned before adding the other ingredients. By browning the meat the stew takes on a darker colour and the flavour will be more intense. A white stew does not involve a preliminary browning of the meat, this results in a lighter tasting and lighter coloured stew.

Choosing Meat or Poultry

Beef

When choosing a piece of beef it should be a light red colour and slightly elastic, without too much gristle. Old beef appears dark in colour and the fat is often yellowish: avoid beef of this type.

There are many different cuts of beef, and each is suitable for different methods of cooking:

Roasting

Topside	Sirloin
Fillet	Ribs
Rump	

Grilling or Frying

Sirloin	Fillet
Rump	Entrecôte

Stewing

Rump	Brisket
Flank	Chuck

Pork

Pork is cheaper than beef and should be a pale pink colour, smooth on the surface and firm. In order to reduce the risk of food poisoning ensure that the pork is cooked through.

Roasting

Ribs	Loin
Leg	Bladebone

Grilling or Frying

Chops	Ribs
Loin	

Lamb

Lamb should be a pinkish red colour, and the bones at the joints should be red.

Roasting

Shoulder	Leg
Best end of neck	Loin

Grilling or Frying

Loin chops or cutlets	Liver

Stewing

Loin	Leg
Breast	Liver

Chicken

Chicken is one of the cheapest of available meats as a result of factory breeding, however they tend to sacrifice flavour in favour of price. If you want to taste how a chicken should taste, try to find a free-range one, available from most stores. When buying chicken it should smell fresh and the flesh should be firm. Chicken is very versatile: most parts can be fried, roasted, stewed etc.

Carving Meat

There is definitely an art to carving, and it does take time to become a proficient carver. The most important thing about carving is having a sharp knife. It is very difficult to try to cut thin slices with a blunt implement. Get into the habit of sharpening the knife before use.

When cutting meat, cut across the grain, this makes it easier to chew, which is important if the meat is on the tough side. The meat should be cut with a gentle sawing action so that straight, whole slices are cut.

Usually when carving roast meat, the juices collect at the bottom of the carving plate. Use these juices when making gravy. When carving a leg of lamb, it can be cut parallel to the bone.

Meat Dishes

Spicy Sausage Casserole

This recipe is perfect for a cold winter's evening. Wash it down with a robust wine with plenty of kick. If you really want to turn up the heat add more chilli powder, or a couple of fresh chillies, or simply put another log on the fire.

Serves 4

Ingredients

1 pack of pork sausages, cut into pieces
1 onion, peeled and chopped
2 cloves of garlic, peeled and finely chopped
1 tin of chopped tomatoes
2 tbs of tomato purée
1 green pepper, deseeded and chopped
Glass of red wine
2 tsp of chilli powder
1 tsp of oregano
2 tbs of oil
Pepper
Salt

Heat the oil in a largish saucepan or wok, then fry the onions, garlic and chilli powder for about 5 minutes. Add the sausages and the pepper, and cook for about 10 minutes. Add the tomato purée, wine, seasoning, tomatoes and oregano.

Simmer for at least 15 minutes then serve with rice and peas. Alternatively, after cooking the rice and peas add them directly to the casserole and cook for another couple of minutes. Also tastes nice with grated cheese on top.

Pork Provençal

This dish is based on a recipe from the Hôtel du Commerce in Castellane. The food and service there is almost as inspiring as the breathtaking scenery nearby. As with most Provençal food there is the usual delectable combination of garlic, onions, tomatoes and herbs.

Serves 4

Ingredients

4 pork steaks/chops
1 onion, chopped and peeled
1 clove of garlic, peeled and finely chopped
1 tin of chopped tomatoes
1 red pepper, deseeded and finely chopped
2 tsp of herbes de Provence
1 finely chopped courgette
4 slices of cheddar cheese
2 tbs of oil
Salt
Pepper

Fry the onion and garlic in the oil for about 5 minutes. When these have cooked, add the tomatoes, red pepper, courgette, herbs, salt and pepper. Let the sauce simmer for 20 minutes. After 10 minutes, grill the pork on foil, turning once. When it is nearly cooked put some sauce and the slices of cheese on the pork and grill until the cheese begins to melt.

Serve with potatoes and fresh vegetables and the rest of the sauce.

Shepherd's Pie

This popular dish is supposed to use leftover beef from a Sunday roast, but minced beef is an adequate substitute for those not indulging in a roast.

Serves 3 to 4

Ingredients

I lb (500g) of minced beef
I onion, peeled and chopped
I clove of garlic, peeled and finely chopped
I tin of chopped tomatoes, (optional)
I tbs of tomato purée
I tsp of mixed herbs
2 tbs of oil
5 medium potatoes, peeled
Butter
Milk
Salt
Pepper

Heat the oil in a largish saucepan, add the onion and garlic, and fry for 3 to 4 minutes. Add the meat and cook for another 10 minutes, then add the other ingredients, (except potatoes, butter and milk) and simmer for 15 minutes.

While this is simmering, cook the potatoes (test them with a knife – the knife should pass through the potato easily), then mash them with a nob of butter and a drop of milk. Put the meat in an ovenproof dish and cover with the potato, then put under the grill until the potato turns a golden brown.

Moussaka

Serves 4

Ingredients

1 large aubergine, sliced
2 large potatoes, parboiled and sliced
2 onions, peeled and chopped
1 tin of chopped tomatoes
1 tbs of tomato purée
1 clove of garlic, crushed and finely chopped
1 lb (500g) of minced beef or lamb
2 tbs of oil
1 oz (25g) of butter
1 oz (25g) of flour
¾ pint (375ml) of milk
4 oz (100g) of grated cheese
Salt
Pepper

Sprinkle the aubergines generously with salt and leave for 30 minutes. Then rinse and pat dry with kitchen paper. Heat a tablespoon of oil in a frying pan and fry the aubergines until they are soft. Then place on a piece of kitchen towel to absorb the fat. Put some more oil in the frying pan if needed and fry the onions, garlic, and meat. After about 10 minutes, season and add the tomatoes and purée.

Grease a casserole dish with either butter or oil, and fill it with alternate layers of aubergine and meat, finishing with a layer of sliced potatoes.

To make the cheese sauce, melt the butter in a saucepan, add the flour, and mix together. Remove from the heat, and very gradually add the milk. Boil until the sauce thickens, then remove from the heat and add 3 oz (75g) of the cheese. Pour the cheese sauce over the top of the aubergine, and sprinkle the rest of the cheese on top.

Bake for 40 minutes on Gas Mark 5 (200 °C, 400 °F).

Sweet and Sour Pork

Serves 4

Ingredients

2 tbs oil
I lb (500g) pork, cubed
I red pepper, deseeded and chopped
I green pepper, deseeded and chopped
2 cloves of garlic, peeled chopped
I courgette, sliced
I onion, peeled and roughly chopped
I tbs dark brown sugar
2 tbs of soy sauce
I tbs of Worcester sauce
3 tbs of tomato purée
2 tbs of wine vinegar
4 tbs of water
Pinch of chilli powder
Salt
Pepper

Heat the oil in a wok or large frying pan and then gently fry the onion and garlic for 5 minutes. Add the peppers, courgettes and fry for another couple of minutes. Take care that none of the vegetables burn. Mix the other ingredients, except for the pork, together in a small bowl or jug, then add to the wok. Add the pork and fry until the meat is cooked. Serve with rice.

Jambalaya

This is perhaps one of the ultimate Cajun recipes. A friend of mine from Louisiana introduced me to a couple of years ago – she used sausages and chicken, although apparently back home she said they also add alligator.

Serves 4

Ingredients

2 tbs of oil
2 chicken breasts, cut into pieces
8 oz (225g) of sausage (chorizo if available)
8 oz (225g) of rice
1 onion, peeled and chopped
2 cloves of garlic, peeled and finely chopped
1 green pepper, deseeded and chopped into pieces
2 sticks of celery, chopped
1 tsp of cayenne pepper
1 pint (600ml) of vegetable/chicken stock
Salt
Pepper

Heat the oil in a large saucepan or a wok. Fry the onions and garlic for about five minutes, add the sausage and chicken and fry for another 5 minutes, then add the pepper and celery. Continue frying for another couple of minutes, then season and add the cayenne pepper. Pour the stock over the top and bring to the boil.

When the stock is boiling add the rice and cook for roughly 20 minutes or until the rice is soft when pinched. Be careful not to overcook the rice.

Chilli Con Carne

If there is one recipe most men can cook then it has to be chilli. The chilli can be made as hot as required, but remember that even though you may love to sweat, your guests might prefer it a little milder. It can be served with rice, potatoes or pitta bread. Chilli tastes pretty good even when cold, and it is not uncommon for me to dig into the leftovers for breakfast. I usually add a green or red pepper.

Serves 4

Ingredients

2 tbs of oil
3 tsp of chilli powder
I lb (500g) of minced beef or stewing steak
I large onion, peeled and chopped
2 cloves of garlic, peeled and finely chopped
¼ pint (150ml) of beef stock
I tin of chopped tomatoes
I tin of kidney beans, drained
I tsp of oregano
I tbs of tomato purée
Glass of red wine, (optional)
Salt
Pepper

After frying the onions, chilli powder and garlic in the oil for about 5 minutes, mix in the mince. Cook the mince for about 10 minutes stirring constantly to stop it burning. Add the other ingredients, except the kidney beans, varying the amounts of seasoning according to taste. Bring to the boil then simmer for

about 20 minutes (the longer the better). 5 minutes before serving add the kidney beans.
Serve with rice or jacket potatoes.

Toad in the Hole

A classic dish that is about as misleading as hedgehog crisps.

Serves 4

Ingredients

1 lb (500g) of sausages
1 oz (25g) of oil
4 oz (100g) of flour
1 egg
½ pint (300ml) of milk
A pinch of salt

Mix the flour and the salt, then make a well in the flour and break the egg into the well. Add the milk slowly to ensure a smooth consistency and beat for a minute or so. Put the sausages in a baking tin covered in the oil and bake for 10 minutes at Gas Mark 7 (450 °F, 230 °C). Add the batter and cook for a further 25 minutes or until the batter has risen and is browned.

Beef Stew

Serves 4

Ingredients

1 lb (500g) of stewing steak
1 onion, peeled and roughly chopped
1 clove of garlic, peeled and finely chopped
1 ½ oz (40g) of flour
1 pint (600ml) of beef stock
3 carrots, scraped and chopped
1 bouquet garni
2 tbs of oil
Salt
Pepper

Put the oil in a casserole dish and fry the onions and garlic for 5 minutes. Cut the meat into 1-inch pieces and roll them in the flour with a little salt and pepper. Fry in a separate pan for 5 minutes or until brown, and add to the onion. Add the rest of the flour to the pan and fry gently. Add the stock and boil until it thickens. Pour the sauce over the meat, add the bouquet garni and carrots, and bake at Gas Mark 4 (350 °F, 180 °C) for one to two hours.

Corned Beef Hash

Serves 4

Ingredients

2 tbs of oil
I tin of corned beef
I large onion, peeled and chopped
Milk
Butter
4 large potatoes
Salt
Pepper

Peel the potatoes and chop them into quarters. Place the potatoes in a saucepan of boiling water and boil for about 20 minutes or until tender. Drain them and mash with a little milk and butter.

Whilst the potatoes are cooking fry the onions in a large frying pan with the oil for about 5 minutes or until they are golden. Open the tin of beef and chop it up into small pieces and add to the onion.

Heat the beef through which will take about 5 minutes and then add the mashed potato. Fry the mixture until the potato turns slightly crispy, but not burnt.

Courgette and Bacon Bake

Serves 4

Ingredients

2 tbs of oil
2 lb (1 kg) of courgettes, sliced
4 oz (100g) of bacon, cut into pieces
5 oz (125g) of grated cheddar cheese
4 eggs
¾ pint (350ml) of milk
Salt
Pepper

Heat the oil in a frying pan then fry the courgettes for 4 to 5 minutes. Then add the bacon and fry for another couple of minutes. Beat the eggs together with the milk, add half the cheese and season. Grease a baking dish and layer the courgettes and bacon until they are used up. Pour the egg and cheese mixture over and put the rest of the cheese on top. Bake at Gas Mark 4 (350 °F, 180 °C) for 40 minutes or until golden.

Lamb Casserole

Serves 4

Ingredients

2 tbs of oil
4 lamb chops
1 onion, peeled and sliced
2 leeks, sliced
8 oz (225g) of carrots, scraped and chopped
4 oz (100g) of peas
1 pint (600ml) of beef/vegetable stock
Salt
Pepper

Heat the oil in a frying pan then fry the chops for a couple of minutes on each side. Add the onion, carrots and leek, and fry for a few more minutes. Transfer into a casserole dish, season, and pour the stock over. Put a lid on the dish and place in the oven on Gas Mark 4 (350 °F, 180 °C) for about 1 hour. Add the peas about 10 minutes before serving.

Roast Dinners

A home-cooked roast dinner is still a favourite and rightly so. If you want to impress, a roast is a good place to start. Choose a nice piece of meat and serve it with fresh vegetables and either new or roast potatoes.

Remember that when using the oven, it should be switched on 20 minutes before the joint is put in, to heat it up to the correct temperature.

Roast Beef

Serves 2 to 20
(according to whether you have a small joint or a whole cow)

Ingredients

1 joint of beef (topside)
¼ pint (150ml) of vegetable oil
Gravy
Salt
Pepper

Before throwing away the packaging for your joint, note how much it weighs. Allow 20 minutes cooking time per lb, plus 20 minutes on top, all at Gas Mark 7 (450 °F, 230 °C). This will cook the meat 'English style', i.e. with little or no blood seeping out. If you prefer it 'rare', cook for about 15 minutes less.

Put the joint in a roasting tin and pour the oil over the top and the sides. Season with the salt and pepper, and stick in the oven.

The joint must be 'basted' – that means to spoon the oil in the tin over the top of the meat to stop it from drying out. Do this two or three times.

When the meat is cooked, carve the joint and serve with fresh vegetables. Gravy can be made from the juices in the roasting tin.

Roast Pork

This must be cooked for a little longer than beef, for it is essential that pork is well cooked. Prepare in the same method as the beef but cook for 25 minutes per lb plus 25 minutes over, on the same oven setting. Baste the joint every 20 minutes. If you like garlic place pieces of garlic into the joint before cooking.

Roast Chicken

It is important not to overcook chicken as it loses all its flavour and is harder to carve.

Place the chicken in a baking tin with ¼ pint of oil and season with plenty of black pepper. Bake for 15 to 20 minutes per lb plus 20 minutes on Gas Mark 6 (425 °F, 225 °C).

Roast Lamb

Lamb is expensive but has a wonderful flavour that makes it worth splashing out on occasionally. Unlike pork, it can be served pink in the middle.

Prepare in the same method as the beef and cook for 20 minutes per lb and 20 minutes extra on the same oven setting. Baste every 20 minutes. Place sprigs of fresh rosemary on the lamb for added flavour.

Chicken Dishes

Stuffed Chicken

Serves 4

Ingredients

2 tbs of olive oil
4 chicken breasts
Juice of one lemon
2 cloves of garlic, peeled and finely chopped
2 tsp of herbes de provence
Boursin cheese
Pepper
Salt

Marinate the chicken breasts in the oil, lemon juice, herbs, garlic, salt and pepper for at least 4 hours. Remove the chicken from the marinade and make a split the length of the breast and stuff with the cheese. Place the chicken breast in an ovenproof dish and pour over the marinade, then sprinkle liberally with herbs.

Place in the oven and cook for 45 minutes on Gas Mark 6 (125 °F, 220 °C). Delicious served with Dauphinoise potatoes and a green salad.

Spicy Chicken

Serves 4

Ingredients

2 tbs of oil
4 chicken portions, skinned
1 clove of garlic, peeled and finely chopped
2 large onions, peeled and chopped
¼ pint (150 ml) of soured cream
1 tbs of paprika
¼ pint (150ml) of chicken stock
Salt
Pepper

Heat the oil in a casserole dish and fry the onions and garlic slowly for about 5 minutes. They should end up golden coloured. When cooking onions do not have the heat up too high as in a manner of seconds the onions can burn. When the onions are cooked add the chicken and paprika and continue to fry for a few minutes. Season, mix in the stock and simmer for 30 minutes.

Just before serving, stir in the soured cream. Serve with rice or potatoes.

Coq au Vin

This legendary recipe is another that suits a cold winter's evening. It is traditionally made using red wine from the Burgundy region of France. Burgundy produces some of the finest wines in the world, but they come at a price, usually a high one. If you are on a budget use a robust wine from a cheaper region. It doesn't really matter where you get your coq from.
Serves 4

Ingredients

2oz (50g) butter
3lb (1.5kg) chicken, jointed
10 shallots
1 tbs flour
8 oz (225g) small mushrooms
4 oz (100g) streaky bacon, chopped
3 cloves of garlic, crushed
½ pint (300ml) red wine
3 tbs brandy
¼ pint (150ml) chicken stock
1 bouquet garni
1 tbs fresh chopped parsley
Salt
Pepper

Beurre Manie
2 tbs butter
2 tbs flour

Melt the butter in a large casserole dish then fry the chicken pieces for 5 minutes, remove from the dish and set aside. Fry the onions, mushrooms, garlic and bacon for 5 minutes then return the chicken pieces. Pour over the brandy and set alight. Pour in the red wine, stock, bouquet garni, and seasoning, then bring to the boil. Simmer for about 2 hours. Whilst the chicken is simmering prepare the beurre manie as follows. Mix the flour and the butter together to form a soft paste. Then add the beurre manie in small pieces stirring constantly as they are added. Remove the bouquet garni before serving and garnish with the parsley.

Coconut and Chicken Soup

Serves 4

Ingredients

2 tbs of oil
3 chicken breasts
I pint (600ml) of water
3 oz (75g) of soluble coconut
I small red chilli
I stalk of lemon grass
½ tsp of curry powder
2 oz (50g) of fresh ginger
4 tbs of cream, (optional)
Fresh coriander
Pepper
Salt

Remove the skin from the chicken, then chop into bite-sized pieces. Heat the oil in a large saucepan and fry the chicken for about 5 minutes, turning frequently to stop it sticking to the pan.

Using a sharp knife, remove the outer layer of the ginger and then slice it into thin pieces. Chop the chilli finely, and remove the outer of the lemon grass and also chop. Add the ginger, chilli and lemon grass to the chicken and fry gently for 3 to 4 minutes. Add the curry powder and seasoning to the chicken.

Dissolve the coconut in the water – it is easier if the water is hot. Add the coconut to the other ingredients, bring to the boil, then simmer for 15 to 20 minutes. The cream should be stirred in 5 minutes before serving.

Garnish with fresh coriander.

Serve the soup with a side order of rice.

Chicken in Wine

Serves 4

Ingredients

2 tbs of oil
4 chicken pieces
1 large glass of red or white wine
2 onions, peeled and chopped
½ pint (300ml) of vegetable stock
2 tbs of flour
Pepper
Salt

Put the flour in a dish and roll the chicken pieces in it until they are evenly covered. Heat the oil in a large saucepan then fry the onions for 5 minutes or until they are golden.

Add the chicken pieces and fry for another 5 minutes. Add the stock, onions, salt, pepper and of course the wine, and simmer for 45 minutes.

Chicken Tandoori

Making your own tandoori will cost much less than buying from a takeaway or even a supermarket.

Serves 4

Ingredients

4 chicken pieces – breast, thigh or wing
1 tbs of tandoori powder
1 clove of garlic, peeled and finely chopped
½ pint (300ml) of plain unsweetened natural yoghurt

Remove the skin from the chicken and make some small incisions in the flesh with a sharp knife.

Mix the garlic, tandoori powder and yoghurt together, then rub some of the mixture into the incisions to allow the marinade to penetrate deep into the chicken.. Leave the chicken in the marinade for at least 3 hours, turning occasionally. The longer it is left the more flavour it will gain.

Cook under a medium heat grill for about 20 minutes, spooning on some more marinade at the same time. Turn the chicken over every few minutes to prevent burning.

Chicken Risotto

Serves 4

Ingredients

1 oz (25g) of butter
1 onion, peeled and chopped
1 clove of garlic, peeled and finely chopped
6 oz (150g) of chicken, cut into pieces
8 oz (225g) of rice
2 oz (50g) of mushrooms
1 pint (600ml)) of chicken stock

Heat the butter in a large saucepan and fry the chicken pieces for 5 minutes. Remove from the pan and put in a bowl. Fry the onion and garlic for 3 to 4 minutes.

Put the rice in a sieve and wash under cold water to remove the starch. Then add the rice to the onions and fry gently for a couple more minutes. Prepare the stock using boiling water, then add a third of it to the saucepan.

After the stock has been absorbed by the rice, add the remaining two-thirds and simmer until the rice is cooked. When the rice is cooked add the chicken and mushrooms and cook for a minute or so, to heat them through.

Chicken with Garlic

This title is bit of an understatement, perhaps it should read, garlic with chicken. Whole cloves are roasted alongside the chicken and when cooked, the cloves can be eaten whole. As they have been cooked for so long they lose their strong aroma, however they take on a unique flavour that is delicious.

Serves 4

Ingredients

1 lb (500g) garlic
3 lb (1.5kg) chicken
2 oz (25g) butter
Juice of one lemon
Salt
Pepper

Peel half of the garlic cloves and keep the rest in their skins. Season the chicken inside and out with salt and pepper, then pour the lemon juice over the chicken, again inside and out. Stuff the peeled garlic inside with half of the butter. Smear the remaining butter over the chicken and place with the breastside down in a baking tray. Cook for 30 minutes. Remove from the oven and place the unpeeled garlic cloves around the edge of the chicken and return to the oven. After another hour, turn the chicken onto its back and cook for a further 30 minutes.

Serve the chicken with the juices from the pan. The whole garlic cloves can be eaten using your fingers, or spread onto toast. Gas Mark 4 (350 °F, 180 °C)

Chicken Curry

Serves 4

Ingredients

2 tbs of oil
4 chicken pieces
2 onions, peeled and chopped
2 cloves of garlic, peeled and finely chopped
3 tsp of curry powder
1 tsp of garam masala
2 fresh green chilli peppers, chopped into rings
1 tin of chopped tomatoes
3 whole green cardamom pods
2 tbs of freshly chopped coriander
1 small pot of natural yoghurt
1 to 2 tbs of water
Salt
Pepper

Heat the oil in a large saucepan, then fry the onion and garlic gently for 5 minutes or until they have softened. Add the curry powder, garam masala and chillies, and fry for a couple more minutes.

Add the chicken and water and fry for 5 minutes. After this the other ingredients can be added, apart from the yoghurt, which is added 5 minutes before serving. Season to taste. Simmer for 30 to 40 minutes, then serve with rice.

Chicken in Beer

The temptation is always to leave out the chicken from this recipe, but aim for restraint.

Serves 4

Ingredients

2 tbs of oil
4 chicken pieces, breast, leg or thigh, etc
1 onion, peeled and chopped
3 carrots, scraped and chopped
1 leek, sliced
4 oz (100g) of mushrooms, sliced
1 large can of your favourite lager
Salt
Pepper

Put the oil in a casserole dish, then fry the onion for 3 to 4 minutes, add the chicken and fry for another 10 minutes. Chuck the rest of the ingredients into the dish then stick into the oven for 1 hour on Gas Mark 5 (400 °F, 200 °C).

Proceed to drink the rest of the beer, taking care not to get so drunk that you forget to take the chicken out of the oven, or at least switch the oven off.

Lemon and Basil Chicken

Serves 4

Ingredients

3 tbs of olive oil
4-8 chicken pieces, breast, leg or thigh, etc
1 glass of white wine
Handful of basil leaves
Juice of 1 lemon
Pepper

Place the chicken in a oven-proof casserole dish and add the lemon juice and oil. Place in a preheated oven on Gas Mark 6 (425 °F, 220 °C) for about 20 minutes. Remove from the oven and add the wine. Return to the oven for a further 15 minutes. 5 minutes before serving add the basil.

Serve with rice or a crisp salad.

Chicken with Mushrooms and Peppers

Serves 4

Ingredients

2 tbs of vegetable oil
4 chicken pieces, breast, leg or thigh, etc
1 green pepper, deseeded and sliced into rings
4 oz (100g) of mushrooms, washed and sliced
1 pint (600ml) of chicken stock
1 onion, peeled and chopped
Salt
Pepper

Heat the oil in a medium-sized saucepan, then fry the onions and chicken for about 5 minutes. Stir in the mushrooms, peppers and seasoning and continue to fry gently for another 10 minutes. Pour the chicken stock over the top and simmer for 30 minutes. Serve with potatoes or rice.

Pasta Dishes

There are several things that people associate with Italy: Pavarotti, football, bad driving, women who always wear sunglasses (even in the dark), and pasta. The Italians are passionate about most things; food is undoubtedly of great importance and is reflected in everything they do. Pasta is the basis of many Italian dishes and its popularity has spread all over the world. Not only is pasta extremely versatile it is also not particularly fattening, it is only the sauces that are fattening!

Fresh pasta is worth buying if you are cooking pasta for a special occasion as it tastes wonderful. Or alternatively why not buy a pasta machine and make your own fresh pasta?

Pasta is normally served with a sauce, and here the imagination can really run wild. Once you have mastered some of the foundation sauces, such as a basic tomato sauce, you can go on to create your own which will give you even more satisfaction.

Cooking Pasta

Allow roughly 2oz (50g) of pasta per person.

Correct cooking of the pasta is essential. After the water has boiled add a good pinch of salt. Long pasta such as spaghetti should be eased gently into a pan making sure that it is not broken. Adding a few of drops of olive oil can prevent the pasta from sticking together. Pasta should be cooked with the lid off, and stirred occasionally.

Normally, dried pasta requires 8 to 12 minutes in boiling water, check on the back of the packet. While it should have some 'bite' to it (al dente), make sure that the pasta is not undercooked, as this could result in indigestion.

If you are cooking fresh pasta it normally only requires 2 or 3 minutes, so watch it carefully. There is a fine line with fresh pasta, with one minute it being perfect, then the next it is overcooked. Don't always go by the recommended time, taste the pasta whilst it is cooking. If you overcook your pasta it will stick together and will taste very doughy.

With most pasta recipes, there is a certain degree of flexibility with the type of pasta that can be used (although it is a bit tricky trying to produce lasagna with spaghetti).

Pasta Sauces

When producing sauces they should be reduced in volume to increase the intensity of the flavour. Do not boil rapidly but simmer gently.

Tomato Sauce (for pasta dishes)

This is basis of many pasta sauces, so master this before you try anything complicated.

Serves 3 to 4

Ingredients

2 tbs of olive oil
1 large onion, peeled and chopped
2 cloves of garlic, peeled and finely chopped

1 tin of chopped tomatoes
1 tbs of tomato purée
2 oz (50g) of Parmesan cheese
6 fresh basil leaves or 1 tsp of dried oregano
Salt
Pepper

Heat the oil in a saucepan, then add the chopped onion and garlic and fry gently for 3 to 4 minutes or until the onions have turned almost translucent. When these have softened, add the tomatoes, purée, herbs, salt and pepper. Cook for another 20 minutes until they have been reduced, then add the cheese if required.

Serve with a pasta of your choice.

Tomato and Tuna Sauce

Serves 4

Ingredients

2 tbs of olive oil
1 medium onion, peeled and chopped
1 clove of garlic, peeled and finely chopped
2 oz (50g) Parmesan, finely grated
1 tin of chopped tomatoes
1 tbs of tomato purée
1 tin of tuna
1 tsp of oregano
1 tsp of brown sugar
Salt
Pepper

Heat the oil into a medium-sized saucepan and fry the onions and garlic for about 5 minutes. Add the tomatoes, purée, oregano, salt, pepper, sugar. Simmer for about 15 minutes or until the sauce has been reduced, then add the tuna and simmer for a further 5 minutes.

Serve with a pasta of your choice and sprinkle with Parmesan.

Pasta with Sausage

Serves 4

Ingredients

4 thick spicy sausages
14 oz (400g) tagliatelle
1 oz (25g) butter
Olive oil
2 oz (50g) finely grated Parmesan
1 clove of garlic, peeled and crushed
1 courgette
2 tbs fresh basil
2 tbs fresh chives
2 tbs fresh parsley
Salt
Pepper

Grill or fry the sausages until cooked then cut into slices. Cook the pasta with a drop of olive oil added to the water to stop it sticking together. Cut the courgette into thin strips so that they look like matchsticks and fry in a little olive oil with the garlic for a couple of minutes. Finely chop the herbs. When the pasta is cooked, drain and return to the pan. Throw in the cheese, herbs, sausage and butter, mix thoroughly and season. If the cheese has not melted return to the heat for a minute.

Spaghetti Bolognese

There are many variations of the recipe, this is my preferred one.

Serves 4

Ingredients

2 tbs of oil
1 lb (500g) of minced beef
1 onion, peeled and chopped
1 tin of chopped tomatoes
4 oz (100g) of mushrooms, washed and sliced
2 cloves of garlic, finely chopped
1 carrot, grated
2 rashes of bacon, cut into small pieces
Glass of red wine, (optional)
2 tbs of tomato purée
¾ pint (350ml) of beef stock
2 tsp of oregano
Salt
Pepper

Put the oil into a large saucepan and heat. Add the onions and garlic, and fry gently for 5 minutes, being careful not to burn them. Add the minced beef and continue frying for a further 10 minutes. Combine the other ingredients.

After your sauce has reduced, which takes around 20 minutes, serve with a pasta of your choice – it doesn't have to be spaghetti.

Carbonara

I'm not sure if this is the traditional recipe for the dish, but it tastes good to me.

Serves 3 to 4

Ingredients

1 tbs of oil
4 rashers of streaky bacon, cut into small pieces
4 egg yolks, beaten
3 oz (75g) of grated Parmesan cheese
6 tbs double cream
Lots of fresh black pepper
A pinch of salt

Boil the pasta in a saucepan for about 15 minutes or for however long it recommends on the packet (I prefer to use tagliatelle with this dish). 5 minutes before the pasta is cooked, fry the bacon in the oil for 4 to 5 minutes.

When the pasta is cooked, strain and then return to the pan. Mix in the cheese, bacon, eggs, cream and seasoning. Heat gently for about a minute until the cheese has melted, then serve immediately with more black pepper.

Lasagne

This is one of everybody's favourite Italian dishes. See the vegetarian section for an alternative recipe.

Serves 4

Ingredients

2 tbs of oil
1 large onion, peeled and chopped
2 cloves of garlic, peeled and finely chopped
1 lb (500g) of minced beef
1 tin of chopped tomatoes
¼ pint (150ml) of beef stock
2 tbs of tomato purée
2 tsp of oregano
Salt
Pepper
1 packet of lasagne (the "no pre-cooking required type")

For the sauce:
1 oz (25g) of butter
2 oz (50g) of flour
1 pint (600ml) of milk
6 oz (150g) of cheese, grated

After heating the oil in a large saucepan add the onion and garlic and cook for 5 minutes. Add the mince and cook thoroughly. Then add the tomatoes, oregano, beefstock, tomato purée and seasoning. After bringing to the boil, simmer for 15 to 20 minutes.

While the meat sauce is reducing, prepare the cheese sauce. Melt the butter in a saucepan and then add the flour, stirring constantly. Remove from the heat and add the milk in stages. If the milk is added in one go, you end up with lumps (in the sauce). After adding the milk, bring to the boil and add the cheese, saving a bit for the top. Then simmer for 3 or 4 minutes; the sauce should now begin to thicken.

OK, so your sauce has not thickened: don't panic! Try adding a bit more flour, but sieve it first if you can. Lumpiness can be rectified by pouring the mixture through a sieve.

Find a shallow baking dish and grease it, then add a layer of meat sauce followed by a layer of lasagne pasta, followed by a layer of cheese sauce. Continue this formation until you have used up your mixtures, making sure you finish with the cheese sauce. As well as sprinkling cheese on top, fresh tomato can be added.

Bake on the middle shelf of a preheated oven at Gas Mark 6 (425 °F, 220 °C) for 30 to 40 minutes.

Pizza

Pizza Marguerita

This is the basic pizza, If you want to design your own, begin with this and add your own toppings.

Serves 1

Ingredients

1 pizza base
Tomato purée
1 tsp of olive oil
1 oz (25g) of grated cheese
Pinch of oregano
Pepper

Spread some tomato purée on top of the pizza base. A thin layer will do – if you put too much on, your pizza will become soggy. Place the cheese on top, season, add the herbs and drizzle on the oil. Bake in the oven until the cheese turns a golden brown colour. It should take roughly 15 minutes on Gas Mark 7 (450 °F, 230 °C).

Pizza Perugia

Serves 1

Ingredients

1 pizza base
Tomato purée
1 tsp of oil
1 oz (25g) of grated cheese
2 oz (50g) of tuna
2 to 3 onion rings
Pinch of oregano
Pepper

Spread some tomato purée on the pizza base. Place the tuna on the purée, then the onion rings and finally the cheese. Season and add the oregano and oil and cook as for Marguerita.

Fish

Fish are particularly nutritious and low in fat so they are ideal as part of a diet. They make a good source of protein, calcium and phosphorous and oily fish contain valuable vitamin D. Although many fish are far from cheap, certain kindssuch as herrings and fresh mackerel are extremely good value.

If a recipe uses a whole fish it will need cleaning. Rather than give it a bubble bath, the head, gills and innards have to be removed. Normally fish come already 'cleaned', but if they don't, ask the fishmonger to do it for you.

Look for the following qualities when choosing fish:

• It should not smell.

• The eyes should be bright and full. If the fish is not so fresh the eyes will be dull.

• The gills should be slime-free, clean and shiny.

• If you press a fresh fish with your finger, the flesh should spring back up.

Fresh fish should be eaten on the day of purchase. Frozen fish does not tend to have as full a flavour as fresh fish. It is, however, useful to keep a couple of cod fillets in the freezer as they can be cooked fairly quickly and easily.

There are several ways of cooking fish, depending on the type of fish and what sort of flavour is required. The most popular methods are baking, poaching, frying and grilling.

Baked Fish with Ginger

Serves 1 to 2, depending on size of fish

Ingredients

1 whole fish, such as red snapper
1 clove of garlic, peeled and finely chopped
1 tsp of soy sauce
Juice of 1 lemon
1 oz (25g) of fresh ginger, peeled and thinly sliced

Place the fish on a piece of foil. Mix the lemon juice, soy sauce, garlic and ginger together and pour over the fish. Seal the fish in tinfoil and bake in the oven for 45 minutes at Gas Mark 5 (400 °F, 200 °C).

Halibut Casserole

Serves 4

Ingredients

2 tbs oil
4 halibut steaks
1 onion, peeled and chopped
½ pint (300ml) white wine
1 garlic clove, peeled and crushed
1 tbs cornflour
8 oz (225g) tomatoes, skinned, deseeded and chopped
1 tbs tomato purée
Salt
Pepper

Heat the oil in a casserole dish. Add the onion and garlic and fry gently for 3 to 4 minutes. Stir in the cornflour, tomatoes, tomato purée and the wine. Bring slowly to the boil, stirring constantly, then add the fish and simmer for 10 minutes or until the fish is cooked.

Cod and Onion Bake

Serves 4

Ingredients

4 pieces of cod or any white fish
1 large onion, peeled and sliced into separate rings
3 sliced tomatoes
2 oz (50g) of butter

This is an easy dish that should take no more than 5 minutes to prepare. Put the fish and onion into an ovenproof dish with the butter, and bake for 20 minutes on Gas Mark 5 (400 °F, 200 °C). Add the sliced tomatoes and cook for a further 10 minutes.

Serve with potatoes and fresh vegetables.

Kedgeree

Serves 4

Ingredients

1 egg
8 oz (225g) of rice
8 oz (225g) of smoked haddock fillet
2 oz (50g) of butter
Juice of 1 lemon
Pepper
Salt

Cook the fish by baking it in the oven for 25 minutes. Then remove from the oven and 'flake fish', removing all bones and skin. Boil the rice according to the instructions on the packet.

Drain and rinse the rice in boiling water – this gets rid of most of the starch. Hard boil the egg by boiling it for 10 minutes. Then cool, remove the shell and chop into pieces.

Melt the butter in a saucepan and add the fish. Cook the fish for 3 to 4 minutes to reheat it. Stir in the lemon juice, chopped egg, seasoning and rice and serve immediately.

Thai Fish Cakes

Serves 4

Ingredients

Vegetable oil
8 oz (225g) cooked cod
8 oz (225g) mashed potato
1 oz (25g) melted butter
1 egg, beaten
1 red chilli
1 spring onion
2 cloves of garlic
Ginger, chopped and peeled
Dried breadcrumbs
1 tbs chopped coriander
Salt
Pepper

Remove the skin and bones from the fish and flake. Mix the fish, potato, and other ingredients together. Shape into cakes by hand. Dip the fish cakes into the egg mixture then roll in the breadcrumbs. Shallow fry in hot fat until they are a golden brown on both sides.

Baked Trout

Serves 2

Ingredients

2 small trout
1 onion, peeled and finely chopped
1 carrot, peeled and finely chopped
1 clove of garlic, peeled and finely chopped
1 oz (25g) of flaked almonds
½ oz (15g) of butter
Salt
Pepper

Melt the butter in a frying pan, then add the onion, carrot, and garlic. Fry for about 5 minutes. Place each trout on a piece of tinfoil, making sure the foil is big enough to completely wrap the fish. Divide the vegetables between the two fish, placing the vegetables on the top and the sides of the fish, sprinkle with the almonds, season and pour over the butter sauce then seal up the tinfoil parcels.

Bake in the oven for about 20 minutes or Gas Mark 5 (200 °C, 400 °F).

Serve with potatoes, rice or salad.

Vegetarian Dishes

Over the past decade the interest in vegetarian food has escalated to a point where it is usual for most people, whether vegetarian or not, to eat certain meat-free recipes in their normal diet.

Whatever the reason for becoming a vegetarian it is a misconception that vegetarian cooking is boring.

Piperade

This is one of those dishes that is quick and easy to prepare and is suitable for a light lunch or supper. The dish originates from the Basque country. Add a pinch of paprika if you want it with a little bite.

Serves 4

Ingredients

2 tbs butter
6 eggs
2 red peppers, deseeded
2 green peppers, deseeded
2 cloves of garlic, peeled and chopped
6 tomatoes, skinned
1 tbs chopped fresh basil
Salt
Pepper

Cut the peppers into strips and chop the tomatoes. Heat the butter in a frying pan and cook the peppers for 10 minutes. Add the chopped tomatoes, garlic, basil and seasoning and cook until the tomatoes are almost to a pulp. Take care that the vegetables do not burn. Whilst the vegetables are cooking, beat the eggs in a bowl. When the vegetables are ready add the eggs to the pan. Stir the mixture until it thickens, but do not let the eggs set completely. This dish is traditionally served with slices of fried ham.

Stuffed Marrow

Serves 4

Ingredients

3 tbs of oil
1 large marrow
1 onion, peeled and chopped
8 oz (225g) of rice
1 tin of chopped tomatoes
3 oz (75g) of mushrooms, chopped
Bunch of parsley
1 tsp of mixed herbs
Salt
Pepper

Wash the marrow then cut a lengthways slice off the top. Using a large spoon, remove the seeds. This should create a substantial hollow. Sprinkle the inside of the marrow with salt then turn it upside down.

Heat the oil in a large frying pan and fry the onion for about 5 minutes. Add the rice and cook for another couple of minutes. Now add the other ingredients except the marrow, adding a few tablespoons of water if needed. Cook for 15 minutes. Rinse the marrow with water and then shake dry. Fill the marrow with the contents of the frying pan then replace the top and wrap in foil.

Bake on the middle shelf of the oven at Gas Mark 4 (350 °F, 180 °C) for about 80 minutes. It might take longer depending on the size of the marrow. Once a skewer can pass easily through the flesh of the marrow it is ready to be served.

Aubergine Bake

Serves 4

Ingredients

2 tbs of oil
1 large aubergine, thinly sliced
2 onions, peeled and chopped
2 cloves of garlic, chopped
5 oz (125g) pot of natural yoghurt
1 tin of chopped tomatoes
1 tbs of tomato purée
1 tsp of dried oregano
3 oz (75g) of grated cheddar cheese
1 oz (25g) of white breadcrumbs
Salt
Pepper

Heat the oil in a frying pan and add the aubergine slices. It is best to cook it in stages because only the bottom of the pan should be covered at any one time. Fry the aubergine until it has softened and slightly browned, then place on kitchen paper to absorb the oil. After cooking all the aubergine, remove it and fry the onion and garlic for 5 minutes.

The next stage is to add the tomato, tomato purée, oregano and seasoning. Bring to the boil, then simmer for 10 minutes before stirring in the yoghurt.

Using a greased ovenproof dish, arrange the aubergine then the tomato sauce in alternate layers. Continue this until the top layer is of aubergine. Cover the top with cheese and breadcrumbs.

Bake at Gas Mark 4 (350 °F, 180 °C), for around 30 minutes. Serve with rice or potatoes.

Macaroni Cheese

This another of my favourite recipes. If you don't have any macaroni use pasta shells.

Serves 4

Ingredients

6 oz (150g) of macaroni
6 oz (150g) of grated cheddar cheese
2 large tomatoes
¾ pint (350ml) of milk
1 oz (25g) of flour or cornflour
1 oz (25g) of butter

Melt the butter in a saucepan and mix in the flour. Gradually add the milk, stirring constantly to prevent lumps. Bring to the boil, add the cheese, then leave to simmer for 3 to 4 minutes.

Now cook the macaroni according to the instructions on the packet. When this is done, drain and mix with the cheese sauce. Put into a baking dish, top with sliced tomatoes and more cheese. Grill until golden.

Vegetable Bake

Serves 4

Ingredients

2 tbs of oil
1 onion, peeled
1 clove of garlic
1 courgette
1 small tin of sweetcorn
1 tin of chopped tomatoes
1 oz (25g) of mushrooms
2 oz (50g) of cheddar
2 slices of bread
1 vegetarian stock cube
Mixed herbs
A slosh of red wine, if available
Salt
Pepper

Pre-heat the oven to (Gas Mark 2, 150 °C. 300 °F). Slice the onion, garlic, courgette and mushrooms, and lightly fry in the oil for 5 minutes. Add the sweetcorn, tomatoes, herbs, seasoning and wine. Mix the stock cube with a cup of water and add to the pan, simmer for about 10 minutes.

If there is a food processor around, use it to turn the bread into breadcrumbs. Otherwise just tear the bread with your bare (but clean) hands. Grate the cheese.

Pour the vegetables into a casserole dish and cover with breadcrumbs and cheese. Put into the oven for 10 to 20 minutes, until the breadcrumbs have gone crispy and the cheese has melted.

Potato and Tomato Cake

Serves 4

Ingredients

2 tbs of oil
2 lb (1kg) of 'old' potatoes
Tin of tomatoes
1 onion, peeled and finely chopped
Salt
Pepper

Heat the oil in a pan and fry the onion gently for 10 minutes then add the tomato, salt and pepper. Keep the heat low and simmer for about 20 minutes so the sauce reduces to a thick liquid. Whilst the sauce is reducing boil the potatoes until they are soft enough to mash. Gradually mix the sauce with the mashed potatoes. When all the sauce is added, spoon the mixture out onto a serving plate and mould into the shape of a cake. Eat hot or cold.

Vegetable Stir-fry

Those fortunate enough to possess a wok will find Oriental cooking a lot easier than those stuck with the indignity of a frying pan. If you do have to use a frying pan, use the biggest one you have. The wok is one of my most used kitchen accessories. Its use does not have to be confined to Oriental cooking.

It is up to you what to put into a stir-fry, though it is often a good way of using up any spare vegetables that are lurking at the back of your cupboard. Experiment with exotic vegetables, oils and pastes.

Serves 4

Ingredients

2 tbs of oil
1 onion, peeled and chopped
1 red pepper, deseeded and chopped
1 green pepper, deseeded and chopped
1 carrot, cut into thin strips
1 clove of garlic, peeled and finely chopped
1 tin of bamboo shoots
1 tin of water chestnuts
1 pack of fresh beansprouts
2 tbs of soy sauce
Salt
Pepper

Pour the oil into your wok, then when the oil is hot, i.e. when it is smoking (try not to set fire to the kitchen in the process), add the onion and garlic, and fry for 5 minutes. If you are using water chestnuts, cook these first as they take the longest to cook, and are nicer when they are slightly crispy. Add the soy sauce, seasoning, and other vegetables except for the beansprouts.

After frying the vegetables for about 5 to 10 minutes, add the beansprouts and cook for a couple more minutes. It is important to keep the beansprouts firm. Serve with rice.

Ratatouille

Serves 4

Ingredients

2 tbs of oil
1 tin of chopped tomatoes
1 onion, peeled and finely chopped
2 cloves of garlic, peeled and finely chopped
1 small aubergine, chopped
1 red pepper, deseeded and chopped
1 courgette, sliced
1 lemon, quartered
2 tsp of herbes de Provence
1 bay leaves
A glass of red wine, water or tomato juice, (optional)
Pepper
Salt

While you are preparing the other vegetables, place the pieces of aubergine on a plate and sprinkle them with salt.

After preparing the other vegetables, wash the aubergine pieces then dry them with kitchen paper.

Heat the oil in a large saucepan. Fry the onions and garlic for about 5 minutes, then add the courgette, the aubergines and the peppers. Cook for about 5 minutes before adding the tomatoes, lemon, and other ingredients. Bring to the boil and simmer for 30 minutes.

Vegetable Curry

Trying to produce the perfect curry is not easy unless you have those authentic accompaniments such as wall to wall mauve carpet, with high-backed carpeted chairs, background Sitar music, steaming hot towels that enable one to have a quick wash at the end of the meal and the vital ingredient – half the local rugby team exposing themselves on the table next to you. It's enough to make you choke on your poppadom, but the food is great.

Serves 4

Ingredients

2 tbs of oil
4 potatoes, diced into 1-inch (2.5cm) cubes
1 sliced leek
1 tin of chopped tomatoes
2 sliced courgettes
1 onion, peeled and chopped
2 cloves of garlic, peeled and finely chopped
1 small pot of natural yoghurt
1 tbs of Madras curry powder
1 dried red chilli
½ pint (300ml) of vegetable stock
1 to 2 tbs of water

Heat the oil in a large saucepan then fry the onion, garlic and curry powder for 5 minutes or until they have softened. Add the other ingredients, except the yoghurt, bring to the boil, and simmer for 40 minutes or more. Stir in the yoghurt 5 minutes before serving.

Whilst the curry is simmering, taste it to see if it is to the strength required. If it is not hot enough for your asbestos-lined mouth just add more curry powder.

Serve with rice, preferably pilau or basmati.

Vegetable Kebabs

You do not have to stick to the vegetables suggested in this recipe.

Serves 2

Ingredients

1 oz (25g) of butter
1 red pepper, deseeded and cut into pieces
1 courgette, cut into chunks
1 small onion, peeled and quartered
2 tomatoes, quartered
4 mushrooms, halved or quartered
Salt
Pepper

Thread all the vegetables onto a couple of skewers and daub them with butter, then grill for about 15 minutes.

For a different flavour try adding a tablespoon of runny honey or a dash of soy sauce whilst grilling.

Serve with rice.

Fruit and Nut Pasta

Serves 4

Ingredients

6 tbs of olive oil
14 oz (400g) of pasta
2 cloves of garlic, peeled and finely chopped
2 oz (50g) of sultanas
2 oz (50g) of pine kernels
Pepper

Cook the pasta of your choice according to the instructions on the packet.

Drain the pasta and place in a serving bowl. Pour the oil over the pasta then stir in the garlic, pine kernels and sultanas. Season using lots of fresh ground pepper.

Lasagne

You can use a meat substitute with this recipe, called silken tofu. It sounds like a Greek island, but it tastes a bit better than that. If you can find some, prepare in the same way as the meat lasagne, substituting the meat for tofu.

Serves 4

Ingredients

2 tbs of oil
1 large onion, peeled and chopped
1 red pepper, deseeded and chopped
1 green pepper, deseeded and chopped
1 clove of garlic, peeled and finely chopped
1 leek finely chopped
2 courgettes finely sliced
1 tin of chopped tomatoes
2 tbs of tomato purée
2 tsp of oregano
1 packet of lasagne (no pre-cooking required type)
Salt
Pepper

For the cheese sauce:
1 oz (25g) of butter
2 oz (50g) of flour
1 pint (600ml) of milk
6 oz (150g) of cheese, grated

Heat the oil in a large saucepan and add the onion and garlic. Cook for 5 minutes, then stir in the leek, peppers and courgette, fry gently for another 3 minutes or so. Add the tomatoes, purée, oregano and seasoning. Bring to the boil then simmer for a further 20 minutes. While the vegetable sauce is simmering prepare the cheese sauce.

Melt the butter in a saucepan and add the flour, stirring constantly. Remove from the heat and add the milk in stages. Then bring to the boil and add the cheese, saving a bit for the top. Simmer for 3 or 4 minutes. Add more flour if the sauce refuses to thicken.

Grease a shallow baking dish, then add a layer of tomato sauce, a layer of pasta, a layer of cheese sauce and so on, making sure to end up with cheese sauce on top. Sprinkle over the remaining cheese on top.

Bake in a preheated oven for around 25 minutes at Gas Mark 6 (425 °F, 220 °C).

Crunchy Rice

This recipe is best cooked in a large wok, but a saucepan or a dustbin lid will do.

Serves 2 to 4

Ingredients

2 tbs of oil
2 cups of wholemeal rice
4 cups of water
1 green pepper, deseeded and chopped
1 small tin of sweetcorn
1 onion, peeled and chopped
1 oz (25g) of mushrooms, sliced
1 clove of garlic, peeled and finely chopped
2 oz (50g) of walnuts
1 vegetarian stock cube
1 tbs fresh chopped parsley
Salt
Pepper

Heat the oil in a large frying pan or wok, then fry the onions and garlic for between 4 and 5 minutes. Add the mushrooms, green pepper and sweetcorn and fry for another couple of minutes. Next add the uncooked rice and about four cups of water. Sprinkle the stock cube over and stir frequently. Simmer for about 20 minutes, depending on the type of rice used. Add more water if necessary to stop the rice from drying out.

If the rice is soft when pinched then it is cooked. Add the walnuts a couple of minutes before removing from the heat. Season with salt and pepper and garnish with the parsley.

Hot Vegetable Stew

This is yet another recipe that can be altered to taste and what vegetables are available. If you are not a fan of hot food you can always omit the chilli pepper.

Serves 4

Ingredients

2 tbs of oil
1 onion, peeled and chopped
2 cloves of garlic, peeled and finely chopped
1 pepper, deseeded and sliced
2 courgettes sliced
1 leek, sliced
1 tin (14 oz) of tomatoes
3 potatoes, peeled and diced
Small can of sweetcorn
4 oz (100g) of cooked green lentils
1 green chilli pepper, chopped
Dash of tabasco sauce
1 pint (600ml) vegetable stock
2 tsp of mixed herbs
Salt
Pepper

Heat the oil in a large casserole dish, then fry the onions and garlic adding the chilli and tabasco, for 3 to 4 minutes. Add the courgettes, leeks and peppers and gently fry for a further 10 minutes. Then add the stock and the remaining ingredients. Bring to the boil and simmer for 30 minutes.

Stuffed Peppers

Serves 4

Ingredients

2 tbs of olive oil
4 peppers
I onion, peeled and chopped
I clove of garlic, peeled and finely chopped
I tin (14 oz) tomatoes
2 tsp of tomato purée
4 oz (100g) mushrooms
Glass of red wine
I tbs of chopped parsley
I tsp of chopped rosemary
Dash of lemon juice
2 tbs of breadcrumbs
Salt
Pepper

Cut the tops off the peppers and remove the seeds, then place in boiling water for 3 to 4 minutes. Remove and plunge in cold water.

Heat the oil in a large saucepan, then gently fry the onion and garlic for a few minutes. Add the other ingredients, bring to the boil and then simmer for 10 minutes. Fill the peppers with the mixture, replace the lid of the pepper and bake in the oven for 35 minutes on Gas Mark 6 (425 °F, 220 °C).

Remember to preheat the oven.

French Beans with Garlic

If you have runner beans they can be used instead, provided you can catch them first.

Serves 4

Ingredients

1 lb (500g) French beans
1 clove of garlic, peeled and finely chopped
1 oz (25g) butter
Salt
Pepper

Top and tail the beans then cut in two. Place the beans in a pan of salted boiling water and cook for 10 minutes or until tender. It is important that they are not overcooked as they will lose their colour and flavour. When cooked, drain the beans. Heat the butter in the pan and let it melt, but don't let it burn. Add the garlic and cook for a minute then add the beans and season. Stir the beans to make sure they are evenly coated before serving.

Courgettes can be cooked in a similar way, except they do not need to be boiled, they can be fried gently in the butter with the garlic.

Dauphinoise Potatoes

If I could only eat potatoes cooked one way it would have to be this one. The combination of potatoes and cream is delicious. They go particularly well with dishes such as hot vegetable stew or chicken in beer.

Serves 4

Ingredients

2 lb (1 kg) 'old' potatoes, peeled and thinly sliced
1 large onion, peeled and thinly sliced
2 cloves of garlic, peeled and crushed
½ pint (300ml) double cream
2 oz (50g) butter
Nutmeg
Salt
Pepper

Grease the base and sides of an ovenproof dish, then put alternate layers of onion, potato, garlic, slices of butter, cream, salt, pepper and grated nutmeg in the dish. Finish with a layer of potatoes. Place in a preheated oven at Gas Mark 5 (400 °F, 200 °C) for about 1 ½ hours. If required, freshly grated cheese such as gruyère or parmesan can be added.

N.B. Only a small amount of nutmeg is used on each layer, the flavour must not be overpowering.

Supper and Snacks

There are certain times when you will not be in the mood for cooking an elaborate meal or you might just fancy something light, that is quick and easy to prepare. It is often the case of seeing what ingredients you have and creating a recipe from what is available, however this does not mean combining cornflakes and mango chutney.

Ham and Eggs

This a perfect supper or lunch dish, that takes only a few minutes to prepare.

Serves 4

Ingredients

4 large eggs
4 slices of ham
Tin of chopped tomatoes
Herbes de Provence
Salt
Pepper

Heat the oven to its maximum temperature. Pour the tomatoes into a baking dish then roll up the slices of ham and place on top of the tomato. Break the eggs carefully on top of the ham, sprinkle with the herbs and season. Bake until the eggs are cooked. Serve with hot buttered toast. I always serve this at Christmas using leftovers from a ham. It makes a refreshing change from the usual Christmas fare.

B.L.T.

Otherwise known as a bacon, lettuce and tomato sandwich.

Serves 1

Ingredients

Butter
3 slices of bread
2 rashers of bacon
A lettuce leaf or two
1 tomato
Salt
Pepper

Remove the crusts from the bread, then slice the tomato. Grill the bacon and the bread. Butter the toast, then place a bit of lettuce, some tomato and a rasher of bacon on it. Put a slice of toast on top and then make up another layer as before. Finish with the last piece of toast on top, then cut diagonally across. Add a dash of salt and pepper if required.

To stop the B.L.T. from falling apart you could try skewering it with a cocktail stick. But under no circumstances should you swallow the cocktail stick in your haste to eat your masterpiece – they are not particularly palatable.

Nachos

This is a quick and easy recipe that is perfect for any occasion.

Serves 4

Ingredients

2 tbs of oil
2 cloves of garlic, peeled and finely chopped
2 tsp of chilli powder
1 large onion, peeled and chopped
1 tin of chopped tomatoes
1 large bag of tortilla chips
4 oz (100g) grated cheese
1 tbs of tomato purée
1 green pepper, deseeded and finely chopped
Salt
Pepper

Heat the oil in a large saucepan, then fry the onion and garlic for about 3 to 4 minutes. Add the chilli powder and the green pepper and cook for another couple of minutes. Then add the tomatoes, tomato purée and seasoning and cook for about 15 minutes. The sauce must be well reduced otherwise it will make the chips soggy.

Whilst the sauce is cooking arrange the tortilla chips in a ceramic dish. When the sauce is ready, pour over the chips and finally cover with cheese. Place under a hot grill until the cheese has melted – enjoy.

Spanish Omelette

As there are numerous variations on this meal, don't hold yourself back with what you add.

Serves 4

Ingredients

4 eggs
1 potato, cooked for 10 minutes and chopped
2 tomatoes, sliced
1 oz (25g) of peas
1 onion, peeled and chopped
Mixed herbs
Salt
Pepper

Beat the eggs, season, add the vegetables and pour into a flan dish. Bake at Gas Mark 6 (425 °F, 220 °C) for 15 to 20 minutes or until the mixture ceases to be runny. If you prefer the onions to be a little more cooked, fry them first for a few minutes.

Serve with a green salad.

Pan Bagnat

Serves 1

Ingredients

1 large ciabatta roll
1 tbs olive oil
Wine vinegar
Sliced tomato
Tuna
Sliced egg
1 clove of garlic
Sliced cucumber
3 black olives
2 slices of green pepper
Salt
Pepper

Cut the ciabatta in half and tear out some of the centre to allow room for the filling. Take the clove of garlic and cut in half then rub the inside of the bread with the cut edge. Pour a tablespoon of the oil over the inside. Fill the roll with the rest of the ingredients, pour the remaining oil evenly over, sprinkle a few drops of vinegar, season and put the top back on. Press down on the top of the roll with a degree of force to combine the flavours together. Do not serve immediately as it is best to wait a little while for the oil to penetrate the bread.

Best eaten sitting on the beach, with a cool beer.

Plain Omelette

Serves 1 to 2

Ingredients

1 oz (25g) of butter
2 or 3 eggs
A pinch of mixed herbs
Salt
Pepper

Beat the eggs together in a mixing bowl and add the seasoning. Melt the butter in a frying pan and pour in the eggs. As soon as the eggs start to cook lift up one edge of the omelette with a spatula, tilt the pan and let the uncooked egg run underneath. Continue to do this until the omelette is cooked, then flip it in half and serve on a warmed plate.

Cheese and Tomato Omelette

Serves 1 to 2

Ingredients

1 oz (25g) of butter
2 or 3 eggs
2 oz (50g) of grated cheese
1 chopped tomato
Salt
Pepper

Prepare as above, but add the cheese and tomato before adding to the frying pan.

Eggy Bread

Serves 2

Ingredients

3 eggs
4 tbs of milk
Slices of bread without the crusts
2 tbs of oil
Pepper

Beat the eggs and the milk together and season. Heat the oil in a frying pan. Dip a slice of bread in the egg mixture and then fry for a couple of minutes on each side.

Egg and Cheese Ramekins

Serves 1

Ingredients

2 oz (50g) of grated cheese
1 egg
1 tomato
Salt
Pepper

Grease a small ovenproof dish, preferably a ramekin dish or one that is about 3 inches (7.5cm) in diameter. Put grated cheese in the bottom of the dish and up the sides. Place in a slice of tomato and then the egg, trying not to break the yolk. Add the seasoning and cover with another slice of tomato and more grated cheese.

Bake in the oven for about 15 minutes at Gas Mark 4 (350 °F, 180 °C) or until the eggs are set.

Breakfast

The good old days when breakfast was a true meal appear to be long gone. Breakfast used to consist of eggs, bacon, tomatoes, sausages, kippers and kedgeree, but nowadays this daily dose of grease has fallen from grace. A normal breakfast is now regarded as a slice of toast and a cup of coffee. Of course there are health risks associated with eating a plate of fried food everyday, but it sure tastes good.

Eggs

When choosing eggs there are a number of options. Battery-farmed eggs account for the majority of egg production, but if possible it is preferable to buy free-range eggs or barn eggs.

Scrambled Egg

Serves 2

Ingredients

3 eggs
1 oz (25g) of butter
4 tbs of milk
Pepper

Beat the eggs in a bowl and add the milk and pepper. Melt the butter in a saucepan and add the egg mixture. Stir the mixture as it thickens. Don't have the heat up too high, or the egg will burn and stick to the pan.

Serve on top of hot buttered toast.

Poached Egg

Ingredients

1 egg per person
Butter or margarine

If you're lucky enough to have a 'poacher ring', simply put a knob of butter in, add the egg and cook for about 4 minutes, according to taste. If not then there is a more traditional way of poaching eggs: Boil some water in a saucepan and then, having broken an egg into a cup or mug, slide it into the water. Only put one egg in at a time!

Fried Egg

Ingredients

1 egg
2 tbs of oil

Pour some oil in a frying pan, if you have a non-stick so much the better. Don't let the fat get too hot, otherwise the egg will stick to the pan and bubble. Crack the egg on the side of the pan and plop the egg into the oil. Fry gently for about 3 minutes, basting occasionally.

Special Meals

There are plenty of good excuses for cooking a special meal. It could be a birthday, anniversary, St Valentine's Day, or maybe you just feel like it. Whatever the occasion, a well cooked and imaginative meal will add to the memories. As with most of the recipes in this book, they are not particularly difficult, but remember there is so much more than just the cooking. Equally important is picking out a balanced menu. There is no point in serving 10 courses if you are going to be violently ill at the end of it. There is also no point in serving expensive food such as caviar or foie gras, if you don't really like it. Cook what you and your partner enjoy eating.

Glazed Lamb Chops

The chops need to be marinated for several hours but they only take a few minutes to cook.

Serves 4

Ingredients

1 tbs oil
4 thick lamb chops
2 wine glasses of sherry
1 tbs mint sauce
2 tsp dark brown sugar
Salt
Pepper

Place the lamb chops in a bowl and mix all the ingredients together. Leave the chops to marinate for at least 6 hours in the fridge.

To cook the chops take them out of the marinade. Heat the oil in a frying pan and fry the chops for a few minutes on each side. They should be served still pink in the middle.

When they are cooked, remove from the pan, pour in the remaining marinade and reduce by bringing to the boil. Pour the sauce over the chops and serve with fresh vegetables.

Pork and Cider Casserole

This is a recipe that was inspired by experimentation, however the end result is most pleasing.

Serves 4

Ingredients

2 tbs oil
1 large onion, peeled and chopped
2 cloves of garlic, peeled and finely chopped
1 tin of chopped tomatoes
1 tbs of tomato purée
2 tsp of herbes de Provence
1 green pepper, deseeded and chopped
1 courgette, sliced
4 pork chops
1 pint (600ml) of dry cider
1 mug of macaroni
½ mug of frozen peas
Salt
Pepper

Heat the oil in a large casserole dish, then fry the onion, garlic and green pepper for about 5 minutes. Then add the pork chops and fry on both sides for a couple of minutes. Add the tomatoes, purée, herbs, courgette, seasoning and cider then bring to the boil.

Simmer for about 40 minutes, adding the macaroni about 10 minutes before serving and the peas about 5 minutes after the pasta. Check to see if the macaroni is cooked before serving.

If the casserole begins to get a little dry add some water or more cider.

Beef Stroganoff

Serves 4

Ingredients

1 lb (500g) of fillet steak
1 large onion, peeled and chopped
1 clove of garlic, peeled and finely chopped
4 oz (100g) of mushrooms, sliced
2 oz (50g) of butter
2 tbs brandy
½ pint (300ml) of soured cream
Salt
Pepper

Bash the steak with a rolling pin to flatten it out, but don't get too carried away. Cut into strips ½-inch (1.5cm) wide and 2 inches (5.5cm) long. Fry the steak in the butter for about 3 or 4 minutes, then remove from the pan and put in a bowl.

Fry the onions and garlic for 5 minutes, then add the mushrooms and cook until they have softened. Season and put the meat back in the pan. Cook for about 10 minutes, stirring occasionally to prevent burning.

Before serving, add the soured cream and the brandy and heat through. Do not allow to boil, otherwise the cream will curdle.

Steaks

The most popular steaks are rump, fillet, sirloin and entrecôte. Fillet is the most tender and lean, but unfortunately the most expensive. Rump steak has a wonderful flavour but is not as tender.

Steaks are best grilled or fried:

To grill
Brush the steaks with butter and season with black pepper. Make sure the grill is hot before you cook the steaks. Grill each side for 3 to 4 minutes. If you want the steaks dripping with blood cook for slightly less time or eat raw. If you like your steaks well done cook for about 5 to 6 minutes on each side.

To fry
Heat a small amount of oil, preferably in a non-stick frying pan, wait till the pan gets very hot then put in the steak. Fry quickly for a couple of minutes to seal in the flavour. Turn down the heat, cook for 5 minutes for 'rare', 5 to 7 minutes for medium and 15 minutes for charcoal. Try to turn the steak over only once.

The above times for both grilling and frying will depend on the thickness of the steak.

Serve the steaks with fried potatoes, or new potatoes, a salad or fresh vegetables.

Marinated Chicken

Serves 4

Ingredients

2 tbs of oil
4 chicken breasts
Juice of 2 lemons
2 tbs of sherry or marsala
1 tsp of French mustard
Black pepper

This dish needs to be prepared a little in advance. If you don't have any sherry or marsala, it could be omitted.

Remove the skin from the chicken if it has not already been done. Dice the chicken breasts into bite-sized pieces and put in a small mixing bowl along with the lemon juice, mustard, sherry and pepper. Mix well and leave in the fridge for several hours.

Heat the oil in a frying pan, then gently fry the chicken for about 10 minutes.

The chicken can be served with fresh vegetables of your choice and dauphinoise potatoes.

Desserts

Croissant Pudding

Serves 4

Ingredients

5 croissants
½ pint (300ml) of milk
2 oz (50g) of castor sugar
2 egg yolks
2 oz (50g) of raisins
Vanilla essence
Ground cinnamon
Brown sugar
Butter

Cut the croissants in half lengthways and butter one side. Beat the egg yolks, castor sugar, milk, add two drops of vanilla essence, then put aside. Grease an ovenproof dish and place a layer of croissants on the bottom, then sprinkle with raisins. Continue this until all the croissants are used up. Do not put too many raisins on the final layer as they are liable to burn.

Briefly beat the milk mixture, then pour over the croissants. Sprinkle with cinnamon. Leave to soak for at least 30 minutes.

Whilst the croissants are soaking preheat the oven to Gas Mark 4 (180 °C, 350 °F).

Sprinkle a thin layer of brown sugar over the top of the dish then place in the middle of the oven for 20 minutes. Remove from the oven, add some more sugar and return to the oven for a further 20 minutes.

Pears in Red Wine

Serves 4

Ingredients

4 pears
4 oz (100g) sugar
¼ pint (150ml) red wine
¼ pint (150ml) water
Pinch of cinnamon
1 oz (25g) browned almond flakes

Put the wine, water, sugar and cinnamon in a large saucepan and heat gently until the sugar has dissolved.

Peel the pears, trying not to damage the fruit, and leave the stalks on. Place the pears in the wine and simmer for about 20 minutes or until they are soft. When the pears are cooked remove from the pan and place in a serving dish. Reduce the wine sauce by boiling rapidly. It should become a syrupy consistency. Pour the wine over the pears and when cool, chill in the fridge. Before serving sprinkle with almonds and serve with cream.

Ricotta and Raspberry Crunch

A delicious summer pudding that does not have to be made with raspberries, you could use strawberries, bananas or grapes. Another alternative uses toasted pine-nuts instead of the almonds.

Serves 4

Ingredients

12 oz (300g) Ricotta cheese
8 oz (225g) fresh raspberries
Toasted almonds
Runny honey

Divide the ricotta into 4 bowls and arrange the raspberries around the edge of the cheese. Put about a tablespoon of honey on top of the cheese and then sprinkle with the toasted almonds.

If you find that is a little bitter, either add more honey or dust with castor sugar.

Baked Apples

Serves 1

Ingredients

1 large cooking apple per person
Mincemeat
Brown sugar
Butter

Remove the cores from the apples and stand them in an ovenproof dish. Fill the hole in the apple with mincemeat and a teaspoon of brown sugar. Add a knob of butter on top. Put enough water in the dish to cover the bottom of the apples. Bake at Gas Mark 4 (350 °F, 180 °C) for about an hour.

After an hour test the apple with a skewer. It should be soft. Serve with cream or ice cream.

Raspberry Brûlé

Serves 4

Ingredients

8 oz (225g) of fresh raspberries
½ pint (300ml) of double cream or whipping cream
6 oz (150g) of demerara sugar or golden granulated

Place the raspberries in a shallow ovenproof dish. Whip the cream until thick, (but not too stiff) and spread over the raspberries. Sprinkle sugar over the cream, covering it completely.

Place the brûlé under the preheated grill, until it is dark and bubbling. Remove then allow to cool. Chill in the fridge for a couple of hours. A cheaper version could be made using sliced banana.

Poached Peaches

Serves 4

Ingredients

Tin of peach halves
½ oz (15g) of butter or margarine
2 tbs of brown or golden granulated sugar
1 tbs of brandy or whisky, (optional)

Drain the syrup from the peaches, reserving a small amount. Melt the butter in a saucepan. Add the peaches with the syrup and sugar.

Heat gently for about 5 minutes then stir in any brandy if desired.

If you have any flaked almonds or nuts, a few of these toasted and sprinkled on top taste good.

Biscuits And Cakes

The emphasis of this book is on preparing main meals rather than cakes and biscuits, as cooking main meals will be of more use. However, teatime comes round every afternoon, usually at about teatime, so an introduction to basic cake-making is included. There is nothing fancy or too difficult – I will leave that to others. But baking cakes is not easy; they can often fail to rise for no apparent reason. However, you can't go too far wrong with a good old Victoria sponge.

Victoria Sponge

The Victoria sponge is easy to make and, if eaten when still warm, it is hard to beat. As an alternative add cream between the layers.

Ingredients

4 oz (100g) of self-raising flour
4 oz (100g) of margarine
4 oz (100g) of castor sugar
2 eggs, beaten
Jam

(Two 7-inch/17cm sandwich tins are needed)

Mix together the sugar and margarine until they are smooth in texture. Gradually add the eggs to the mixture, then fold in the flour. Divide the mixture between the two baking tins (these need to be greased first, which means wiping the inside with a piece of greaseproof paper covered with fat). Make sure that the tops of the cakes are level, then bake in the oven for 20 minutes or so at Gas Mark 5 (400 °F, 200 °C).

The way to see if a cake is cooked is to stick a skewer or a clean knife in the centre of the sponge. If bits of the mixture are stuck to it when it is drawn out, it needs to be cooked a little longer. If the skewer comes out clean, the cake is ready.

Now turn the cakes out of the tins onto a wire rack (look in the grill pan for one). Once cooled, spread a layer of jam over one of the layers, sandwich the other one on top, and sprinkle with castor sugar.

Treacle Tart

This can be serve hot or cold, with cream or ice-cream or on its own.

Serves 4

Ingredients

4 oz (100g) plain flour
2 oz (50g) fresh white breadcrumbs
3 tbs water
2 oz (50g) butter
12 tbs golden syrup
2 tsp grated lemon rind
Salt

Add a pinch of salt to the flour and sieve. Cut the fat into small pieces and rub them into the flour until the mixture resembles fine breadcrumbs. Add a tablespoon of water at a time until a firm dough is produced. Cover a clean surface or pastry board with a sprinkling of flour. Roll out the pastry so that there is enough to cover the bottom and sides of an 8-inch (20cm) flan dish. Mix the syrup, breadcrumbs and lemon juice together then spoon into the flan case.

Bake for about 25 minutes at Gas Mark 6 (425 °F, 220 °C), until golden.

Chocolate Crunch

Ingredients

4 oz (100g) digestive biscuits, crushed
4 oz (100g) rich tea biscuits, crushed
4 oz (100g) butter
3 oz (75g) golden syrup
1 oz (25g) cocoa powder
6 oz (100g) plain chocolate
Icing sugar

Using a piece of greaseproof paper dabbed in butter, wipe the inside of a shallow baking tin. I know that using a can of WD40 would be quicker but it probably wouldn't taste as good. Melt the butter in a saucepan and add the syrup and cocoa, mix together then add the crushed biscuits. Remove from the heat. Stir the mixture thoroughly so that the biscuit crumbs are evenly coated. Transfer the biscuit mixture into the tin and press down the mixture using a back of a spoon and leave to cool.

To melt the chocolate, place a Pyrex bowl on top of a pan of simmering water. Do not put too much water in the saucepan as there is a chance the water might boil over the edge. Place the chocolate in the bowl and let it melt. When the chocolate has completely melted remove the bowl from the heat using a pair of oven gloves and pour the chocolate over the biscuit mixture. Spread the chocolate so there is an even coating. Allow to cool then cut into squares or slices. Dust with icing sugar. If the weather is warm they can be kept in the fridge to stop them from melting.

N.B. To crush the biscuits, put them in a clean bag, tie the ends and bash with a rolling pin.

Rock Buns

Ingredients

8 oz (225g) of self-raising flour
4 oz (100g) of margarine
3 oz (75g) of currants or raisins
A pinch of nutmeg
3 oz (75g) of sugar
1 egg, beaten
2 tbs of milk
A pinch of salt

Mix the flour, nutmeg and salt together. Then rub the flour and margarine together until they look like breadcrumbs. The next stage is to add the currants, sugar, egg and milk. The mixture should be fairly firm.

Grease a baking tray with some margarine. Mould the mixture into small lumps and place on the baking tray.

Bake for 15 to 20 minutes, Gas Mark 6 (425 °F, 220 °C).

Chocolate Cake

Ingredients

6 oz (150g) of self-raising flour
6 oz (150g) of margarine
6 oz (150g) of castor sugar
3 eggs
1 ½ oz (40g) of cocoa
1 ½ tbs of water

(For the icing)

8 oz (225g) of icing sugar
4 oz (100g) of plain cooking chocolate
1 ½ oz (40g) of butter/margarine
2 tbs of warm water

Place the sugar and the margarine in a large mixing bowl and mix together, using either a wooden spoon or an electric mixer (which will save time). Add the eggs, one at a time.

In a separate bowl, mix the flour and the cocoa powder together, then fold it into the creamed mixture. Continue mixing, adding water until a soft dropping consistency is achieved.

Divide the mixture equally between two 7-inch (17cm) sandwich tins. Bake in the oven at Gas Mark 5 (400 °F, 200 °C) for 25 to 30 minutes.

Test the cake with a skewer. If the mixture sticks to it, the cake needs a few more minutes in the oven.

When the cakes are ready, turn them out of their tins onto a wire rack (if available). Melt the chocolate by placing it in a basin and putting that over the top of a saucepan of boiling water. Be careful not to let the water boil over the top of the pan into the chocolate.

After the chocolate has melted, allow to cool. Cream together the butter and half the icing sugar, then add half the melted chocolate. Mix, and spread over one side of the cake, then 'sandwich' the two together.

The rest of the chocolate is used to make the icing on the top. Add the water and remaining icing sugar to the chocolate, and spoon onto the top of the cake. Spread the icing around using a palette knife that has been dipped in hot water (this helps to spread the icing and stop it sticking to the knife).

The cake can be decorated with those little silver balls that break your teeth, or with tasteful designs of snooker tables etc.

Flapjacks

Ingredients

8 oz (225g) of porridge oats
4 oz (100g) of margarine
3 oz (75g) of sugar
4 tbs of golden syrup
A pinch of salt

Melt the margarine in a large saucepan, then add the syrup and leave over a low heat for a couple of minutes. Remove from the heat and add the sugar, salt and oats. Mix thoroughly using a wooden spoon, making sure all the oats are covered with syrup.

Grease a shallow baking tray and evenly spoon in the mixture. Cook for 20 to 30 minutes at Gas Mark 4 (350 °F, 180 °C). After cooking, cut the flapjacks into bars before they cool.

Scones

Ingredients

8 oz (225g) of self-raising flour
2 oz (50g) of margarine
¼ pint (150ml) of milk
A pinch of salt

Mix the flour and salt together. The flour is supposed to be sieved, but it can be a bit time consuming and doesn't make much difference anyway. Cut the margarine into small cubes and add them to the flour. Rub the mixture using your fingers, continuing until the result looks like breadcrumbs.

Add the milk and stir in using the blade of a knife to form a soft dough. Roll out the mixture on a floured board until it is about ½ an inch (1.5cm) thick. Cut into rounds using a biscuit cutter or a glass.

Grease a baking tray and place some scones on it, leaving enough room for them to rise. Brush some milk over the top of the scones to obtain a smooth and shiny finish.

Bake in the oven for 10 to 15 minutes at Gas Mark 7 (450 °F, 230 °C).

Cheese Scones

As for above, but stir in 4 oz (100g) of cheese before adding the milk.

Fruit scones

As for plain scones, but stir in 1 oz (25g) of sugar and 2 oz (50g) of dried fruit, sultanas, currants etc.

Batters

Pancakes

Serves 4

Ingredients

4 oz (100g) of plain flour
1 egg
½ pint (300ml) of milk
A pinch of salt
Butter
Sugar (or any other topping)

Put the flour and salt in a bowl and add the egg into the middle. Pour in about a third of the milk. Stir gently, adding a little more milk in the process. Beat the mixture thoroughly, then add the rest of the milk. Stir well, then pour into a jug.

Melt a small piece of butter in a frying pan, then add a couple of tablespoons of the batter. Tip the frying pan to spread the mixture evenly. Fry until the underside is brown, then toss the pancake.

Scrape the mess from the dropped pancake from the floor, then start again. This time, when the underside is brown, turn it over with a fish slice or a knife and cook the other side.

Tip the finished pancake onto a plate and cover with lemon juice and sugar.

Yorkshire Pudding

Serves 4

Ingredients

4 oz (100g) of plain flour
1 egg, beaten
1/2 pint (300ml) of milk, or milk and water
Oil
A pinch of salt

Mix the salt and flour in a mixing bowl, then make a 'well' in the flour and add the egg. Mix together carefully adding the milk little by little. Beat the mixture for a few minutes until it is smooth. Pour a teaspoon of oil into the individual patty tins, then add 2 tablespoons of the mixture into each. Bake for about 15 minutes or until they have risen and browned.

Index

A

B

C

INDEX

INDEX

M

Macaroni Cheese 116
Mange-tout 24
Mayonnaise 33
MEAT 69
Mini Sausages 48
Mint Sauce 39
Moussaka 72
Mushrooms 24
Mushrooms With Garlic 64

O

Oatmeal Herrings 108
Omelette 134

P

Pan Bagnat 132
Pancakes 155
Parsley Sauce 32
Parsnips 25
Pasta Sauces 96
Peas 25
Pepper Salad 61
Peppers 25
Piperade 113
Poached Peaches 147
Pork Provençal 70
Potato And Tomato Cake 117
Pumpkin 27
Pumpkin Soup 56

R

Ratatouille 119
Ricotta And Raspberry Crunch 144

S

Salad Niçoise 60